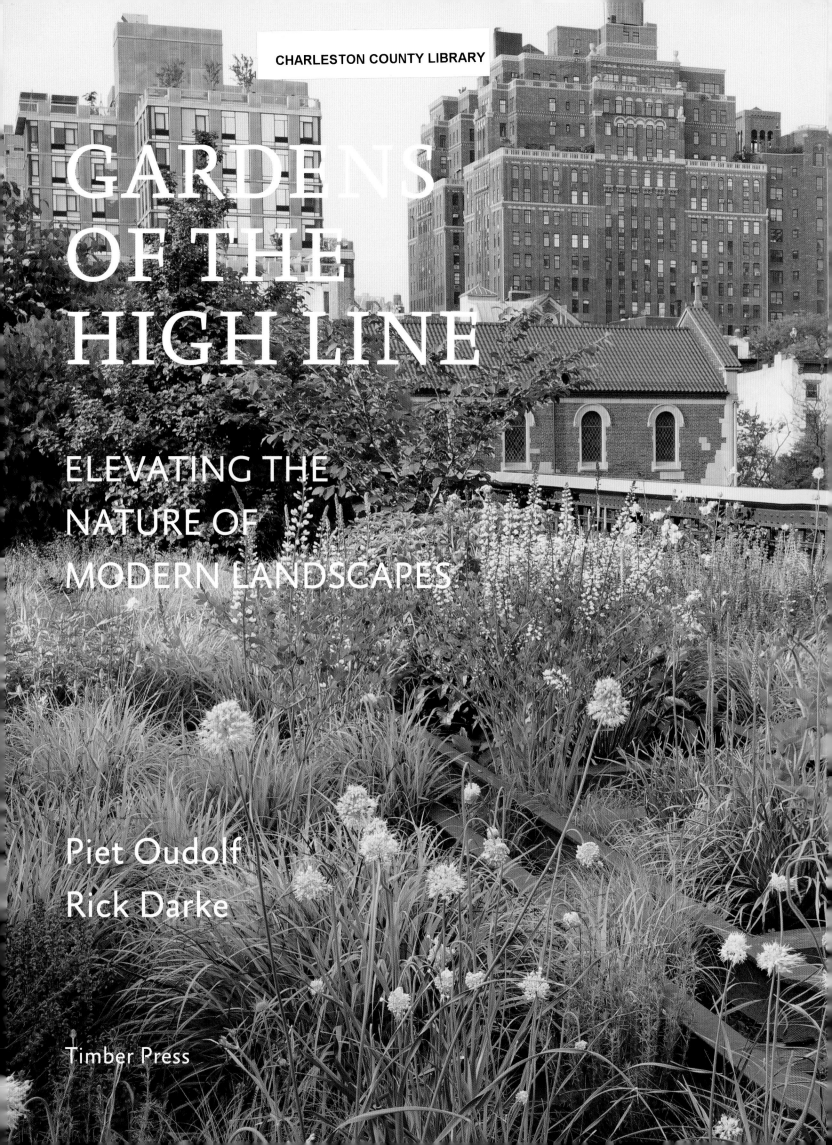

GARDENS OF THE HIGH LINE

ELEVATING THE NATURE OF MODERN LANDSCAPES

Piet Oudolf

Rick Darke

Timber Press

CONTENTS

I feel very strongly
in the sort of
planting that I do,
that you feel the
changes all the time.
It is a changing
beauty: from beauty
into beauty.

— PIET OUDOLF

Chelsea Grasslands, mid-November.

PREFACE

The idea for a book dedicated to the High Line's gardens originated with co-founder Robert Hammond. Robert's offer to write the introductory chapter and provide the support of Friends of the High Line staff added immense appeal to the project. Others who'd played essential roles in making and shaping the High Line also offered to share their knowledge and insights. When our friend and graphic designer Lorraine Ferguson agreed to join us, we felt we had the team needed to produce a book that would portray the gardens beautifully and meaningfully. This is the result of that collaboration.

For readers just discovering the High Line and others who already know it, this book presents a journey through its gardens in all their seasons, illustrating in great detail their design, evolution, care and context. Though the journey can begin at any of the entry points, the original design intention was that it would begin by ascending the Gansevoort stair at the south end and continue north. We've organized this book to match that order.

Robert's introduction is followed by a chapter titled "Elevating the Nature of Modern Landscapes." Its purpose is to assess and illustrate revolutionary developments in industry, urban aesthetics, horticulture and ecology that led to the creation of an unprecedented urban landscape that has unique global resonance. The next section, "Gardens of the High Line," makes up the majority of the book. It begins with a map and follows with chapters devoted to each of the High Line's garden areas. These south-to-north portraits of place are augmented by chapters devoted to the gardens' care, habitat value and seasonality, titled "Cutback," "Gardening," "Life Line" and "Seasons."

We believe, as landscape architect James Corner has suggested, that the High Line in its totality is irreproducible: "You just can't take it anywhere else. Its life, and the energy it has, are drawn in large measure from unique context."[1] At the same time, we know its design ethos, the patterning of its plantings and the enlightened stewardship devoted to them is highly reproducible and broadly worthy of emulation. We hope this book will serve as a beautiful memory of a great place, as guide to the infinite opportunities it presents to practice the art of observation and as an inspiration to all who, publicly or privately, seek to elevate the nature of modern landscapes.

Heart-leaved aster (*Aster cordifolius*), hairy alumroot (*Heuchera macrorhiza* 'Autumn Bride'), Dale's alumroot (*Heuchera americana* 'Dale's Strain') and wild-oat (*Chasmanthium latifolium*) thrive between steel rails and riveted railings at a corner of the Northern Spur in late September.

INTRODUCTION

Robert Hammond

When I first stepped up on the High Line in 1999, I truly fell in love. What I fell in love with was the tension. It was there in the juxtaposition between the hard and the soft, the wild grasses and billboards, the industrial relics and natural landscape, the views of both wildflowers and the Empire State Building. It was ugly and beautiful at the same time. And it's that tension that gives the High Line its power.

Joshua David and I founded Friends of the High Line to try to share that magic. At first we just wanted to keep the space exactly as it was. We would leave all of the plants in place and simply put a path down the railway. It would have been a completely wild garden. That turned out not to be feasible. We had to remediate the structure, removing lead paint and putting in new drainage. This meant we had to take up everything—the rails as well as all of the plants.

So we had to find a new way. We were not architects or planners. We thought New Yorkers should have a say in what happens on the High Line, so we asked the public for their ideas at a series of community input sessions. At one of these sessions, I received a card that said, "The High Line should be preserved, untouched, as a wilderness area. No doubt you will ruin it. So it goes."

I kept that card posted above my desk. Because that has always been my biggest fear. That we couldn't capture that naturalistic beauty in its wild state. That we would ruin it.

Opposite: Early evening light illuminates grasses, seedheads of Queen Anne's lace, and other self-sown plants on the High Line at the Rail Yards in this August 2008 view west to the Hudson River.

Robert Hammond on the High Line in 2007. Photo © Barry Munger, courtesy of the artist.

What New Yorkers fell in love with was a series of photographs by Joel Sternfeld taken on the High Line between 1999 and 2000. These images gave many New Yorkers their first glimpses of that hidden wilderness and helped to catapult the movement to open it as a public space. Just one glimpse of Joel's photography conveys the tension that we wanted in the reconstruction.

With that image in mind, we hosted a design competition, looking for visionaries with more experience and talent than us who could conceive and carry out what the space called for—something as unexpected as the original. And we finally saw it again in the design that James Corner Field Operations, Diller Scofidio + Renfro, and Piet Oudolf created. Drawing on the dynamic community of plants that had crowded the High Line for decades, the team designed a totally new experience that captured the soul of the space.

Other designs we received were either very architectural or tried to exactly recreate the original wild landscape. Neither of those concepts were right. A strictly architectural approach would certainly have sacrificed the magic of the wilderness. The opposite idea, of putting all of

Joel Sternfeld
An Evening in July, 2000, 2000 (printed 2016)
Pigment print, 13¾ x 17½ inches (34.93 x 44.45 cm)
© Joel Sternfeld, courtesy of the artist and Luhring Augustine, New York
This image captures the view looking east on 30th Street.

the wild plants back "exactly" as they had been, though logical at first glance, was too logical. We felt that approach would anesthetize the final effect. It would be like a wax museum of the old elevated tracks.

At the time, I was reading Giuseppe di Lampedusa's *The Leopard* and was struck by the quote, "Everything must change so that everything can stay the same." And that's what this design team did. They didn't try to put something new on the High Line and didn't try to slavishly recreate what was up there before. They created an all-new magic that captured what Josh and I and so many others had fallen in love with.

The High Line of today is not the abandoned field of wildflowers we saw in 1999. It has a new tension. You can see it, in part, in the fact that it is a hybrid space, built on contradictions: it's an art museum on an industrial structure. It's a community space running a mile and a half through several neighborhoods. It's a botanical garden suspended over city streets. Unlike Central Park, it's an immersion in the city, not an escape from it.

But what I'm most often struck by is how clearly that original tension is captured within Piet Oudolf's planting designs. Breaking design tradition, Piet envisioned a multiseason garden of perennials, where the skeletons of plants have as much a part in the landscape as new growth. Throughout the year, tall grasses and reaching flowers grow and fall back like tides. The winter garden is as powerful as the summer, with the texture provided by dry stalks and seedheads. The brown plants against new growth echo the larger contradictions of the High Line: the wilderness in the city, the art museum on a train track. Like the park itself, the gardens hover between beauty and decay.

In many ways, today's High Line plantings are more dynamic than the plants they replaced. On the old tracks, the plants changed gradually through the seasons. In contrast, the High Line gardens change every week. They are filled with native and introduced, drought-tolerant perennials that behave as wildly as their forebearers did. These plants thrive and spread, trying to take over more than their originally allotted space.

Visitors' unscripted responses to the High Line.

This constant change, the tension between beauty and decay, is akin to the energy that drives New York. Like our city, the gardens reveal a dichotomy that becomes a force of inspiration. And people react to it in unexpected ways.

Like using it for dating apps. One of our staff members collected profile photos taken on the High Line for the popular hook-up app for gay men, Grindr. Why do Grindr users choose this backdrop? Like Joel Sternfeld, they see haunting romance and excitement in the contrasts. It's perfect for a clandestine encounter. It's beautiful but still urban not suburban. For maybe slightly different reasons, it's also very popular for engagement photos.

It takes a special kind of gardener, with an artist's eye, to maintain the tension of the High Line. Other designers have a rigid view of how their visions should be tended. But Piet's openness to change and the freedom he gives to the plants elevate gardening on the High Line to an art form.

It requires an incredibly dedicated level of stewardship as well. Just like a minimalist building is harder to design and keep-up than it looks, the gardens require much more care than their wild, natural-looking abundance suggests. For this reason especially, Friends of the High Line is deeply grateful to our members and donors, as their support makes tending to this complex wildness possible.

When people talk about the High Line they talk about the plants, but they also talk about the crowds. One might think I'd look back fondly on the time when I could walk up on the High Line alone. But it's better with people. Josh and I talked about this effect when it opened: it was the people within this landscape that kept it alive, that kept it from being a sterile botanical garden. The people are as important as the perennials. We create a new kind of tension.

Before it was restored, the High Line was a spontaneous wonder. Today, it's something more. The untouched landscape we saw, covered with wildflowers, was surreal. The High Line today is incredible—it's a botanic garden, a central plaza, an art museum, a cultural center and an evolution of the wonder that was hidden in the middle of Chelsea for decades. It's always free. It is a living, changing space where anyone can experience that irresistible tension. And that, even more than wildflowers in the city, is something I never thought could be possible.

Robert Hammond and Piet Oudolf meet with landscape architects James Corner and Lisa Switkin in the middle of the Gansevoort Woodland, immersed in the landscape they created together and equally immersed in the city, May 2016.

I just pray that, if they save the High Line, they'll save some of the wild parts, so that people can have this kind of hallucinatory experience of nature in the city.[2]

    — JOEL STERNFELD

ELEVATING THE
NATURE OF MODERN LANDSCAPES

When asked, "What is most intriguing about the High Line?" a friend answered, "Its contradictions." So true.

The High Line's contradictory nature owes to its origins: a collage of seemingly antithetical elements that together embody an optimistic vision of people and place in changing times. Its gardens rest on a monumental example of America's heavy industry, yet their signature is an extraordinary lightness of being. Rooted in the past, their story is unapologetically forward-looking. There's a deep precision in the gardens' design and management, yet the plants and patterns are ever-evolving, constantly in flux. The soul of the High Line is confident of the enduring essence of good design, the transitory nature of gardens and the ephemeral joys that inevitably follow. Quoting Gaston Bachelard from his book *The Poetics of Space:* "It is better to live in a state of impermanence than in one of finality."[3]

Though the sensual experience of gardens involves scent, sound and touch, it often begins with a visual event that triggers emotion and intellect. Joel Sternfeld's insightful photographs of the wild High Line provided that visual catalyst, speaking to a yearning that was widely felt but previously inarticulate. Joel describes his initial experience of the High Line's landscape as hallucinatory and this speaks to an essential quality present then and now: it is a place for daydreaming. Again taking a cue from Bachelard, daydreaming "transports the dreamer outside the immediate world to a world that bears the mark of infinity."[4]

The contradictory nature of the High Line allows it to be a defining neighborhood place and a cosmopolitan destination. Its gardens belong to Chelsea and they belong to the global community. Their mix of perennials and grasses draws extensively from North America's indigenous prairie flora, yet a majority of these species were first introduced to horticulture through the efforts of gardeners, growers and designers from distant isles and continents. The gardeners who tend them are as planetary in their diversity as the gardens themselves. Unprecedented in their aspirational qualities, the gardens of the High Line have proved relevant to over seven million visitors yearly at current count. Though the High Line will never be duplicated in detail, its elemental values will endure as model for elevating the nature of modern landscapes.

Still beautiful and functional, steelwork designed for the New York Central Railroad now carries the High Line's gardens over 10th Avenue, August 2016.

Gerald K. Geerlings (1897–1998)
Jeweled City, 1931
Etching and aquatint
Sheet 20 9/16 × 15 5/8 inches (52.2 × 39.7 cm); plate 15 9/16 × 11 11/16 inches (39.5 × 29.7 cm)
Whitney Museum of American Art, New York
Purchased with funds from The Lauder Foundation, Leonard and Evelyn Lauder Fund

With the clarity of hindsight, the gardens of the High Line are an elegant solution to an obvious opportunity that remained obscured until an unprecedented awareness of social, economic, industrial and biological trends came into focus. The High Line evolved from epiphany to public garden in a mere decade, but a look at the arc of its origins reveals it was a long time coming. The story begins with the aesthetics of industry.

The days when railroads and steel mills blackened America's noonday skies are long past. The elevated lines ("Els") that once darkened New York City streets and sidewalks are nearly all gone. As these absences free us to look anew at the relict industrial landscape, we become aware of the beauty of its functionality, and "gritty" slowly morphs into "pretty." New York Central engineers designing the High Line knew such beauty: just look at the railings and rivet and plate patterns visible at each street crossing. Period art began celebrating this aesthetic; none more eloquently than Gerald Geerlings's *Jeweled City* (1931). Created the year construction began on the High Line, it depicts rivets sparkling under stars and street lights.

Graphic designer Paula Scher understood how much the High Line's identity derives from the reimagining of industry when she created its logo saying, "The style is industrial

Abstracted from steel rails and wooden ties, the High Line's logo ably represents its landscape and gardens without showing plants.

Above: The High Line crosses 10th Avenue in a snow storm, March 2015.

The restored wild garden at William
Robinson's Gravetye Manor, in West
Sussex near East Grinstead.

Built in 1598 for local iron-maker
Richard Infield and his wife, Katherine,
Gravetye (pronounced *grave-tie*) was
in disrepair when Robinson acquired

it in 1885. For the next fifty years it
served as Robinson's living laboratory
of wild garden experimentation.

rather than gardenlike and that's a deliberate choice. It's about reclaiming industrial territory and reinventing it in a completely modern and urban way. That's the true brand."[5]

The modern, urban nature of the High Line's reinvention will be forever linked to its creative reuse of industrial aesthetics and to the authentic origins of its gardens' naturalism. The High Line isn't the first, isn't even a pioneering example of a wild garden; however, it is the most extraordinary example of a public garden that has grown directly from the living dynamics of its own wild origins.

The wild garden concept first gained traction with the 1870 publication of William Robinson's *The Wild Garden*.[6] Evolving through seven editions in Robinson's lifetime (1838–1935), the book promoted an authentically naturalistic approach that welcomed the vitality and functionality of wild plants into deliberately designed gardens. Robinson had multiple motives for writing *The Wild Garden*. After emigrating from Ireland, Robinson became expert in the native flora of his adopted British Isles and wanted to promote its use in gardens. In *The Wild Garden* he suggests "The passion for the exotic is so universal that our own finest plants are never planted"[7] and then describes many species worthy of cultivation. Yet Robinson was no nativist. His vision of wild gardens was cosmopolitan, promoting a global mix of perennial plants that had one thing in common: they were all capable of thriving in local conditions.

In travels across North America and northern Europe he was continually on the lookout for species that could enhance the beauty and durability of gardens while requiring a minimum of care or resources. Robinson knew that the key to this was in learning how to naturalize plants in the garden, so that they were not entirely dependent upon gardeners for their long-term survival and renewal. Experiments he made at Gravetye, his estate garden in Sussex, England, demonstrated the advantages of managing locally adapted naturalized perennials rather than struggling to maintain poorly adapted plants in fixed patterns.

The nineteenth-century's Industrial Revolution was also partly responsible for Robinson's motivation to develop a more conserving, less maintenance-intensive approach to gardening. Readers of his books included many owners of large estates whose gardens required legions of gardeners for their upkeep. As gardeners left for new jobs in industry it became clear a less time-consuming method of gardening was necessary. The adoption of wild gardening's strategies was both progressive and practical.

William Robinson's groundbreaking classic, *The Wild Garden*, was first published in 1870 in England.

The influence of *The Wild Garden* grew steadily in Robinson's lifetime, extending from Great Britain to Continental Europe and North America. Frederick Law Olmsted owned a copy of *The Wild Garden* and shared Robinson's concepts with Calvert Vaux, with whom he worked on the design of The Rambles in New York's Central Park. The book's concepts have proved increasingly relevant to gardeners worldwide in recent decades, as the potential role of gardens in sustaining regional ecologies has become clearer.

Along with a growing acceptance of wild gardens and a shift from annual to perennial plants, the gardening world's embrace of grasses was a prerequisite for the High Line's planting design and palette. Though grasses are commonly cultivated now, they were considered weeds by most gardeners until recently. A look at gardens well into the twentieth century proves grasses were rarely present except for the occasional specimens of pampas grass (*Cortaderia*), fountain grass (*Pennisetum*), or *Miscanthus*. They were typically set off as curiosities and referred to as ornamental grasses to distinguish them from lawn and turf species.

The stunning grassy diversity that is now a signature of the High Line's gardens has its origins in the work of German nurseryman and garden philosopher Karl Foerster (1874–1970) and his 1957 book *Einzug der Gräser und Farne in die Gärten* (The arrival of grasses and ferns in the garden).[8] In it, Foerster celebrated the unique line, form, translucency and movement grasses bring to the garden. He demonstrated how to mix them in naturalistic arrangements and described how their beauty lingers through winter. Through his writing and nursery offerings, Foerster greatly increased the array of available landscape grasses, including North American species, and influenced generations of northern European gardeners, landscape designers and nurseries.

Europe's growing enthusiasm for grasses eventually reached the United States through increasing international exchange of plants and ideas. Kurt Bluemel, a Sudeten German who immigrated to the United States in 1957, started producing grasses at his Maryland nursery in 1964. Together with former East German landscape designer Wolfgang Oehme, Bluemel brought the European palette of grasses to America and then went on to expand his offering of grasses, sedges and rushes to include unprecedented global diversity. Along with grasses they introduced new broad-leaved perennials from pioneering nursery people including Ernst Pagels and Hans Simon of Germany and Piet and Anja Oudolf of Holland.

Karl Foerster's seminal book *Einzug der Gräser und Farne in die Gärten* (The arrival of grasses and ferns in the garden), originally published in Germany in 1957, influenced gardeners and designers throughout Europe.

A naturalistic composition of grasses and hardy perennials in the restored Foerster garden in Potsdam-Bornim, which is conserved as a monument to his work. Photo by Melinda Zoehrer.

As interest in North American prairie species grew at home and in Europe, collaborative efforts among German plantsmen, including Hans Simon and Cassian Schmidt, and Americans, including Neil Diboll of Prairie Nursery, Roy Diblik of Northwind Nursery, and Dale Hendricks of North Creek Nurseries, brought a new range of grasses and perennials into cultivation. Oehme formed a partnership with landscape architect James van Sweden and together they brought grasses to the attention of the American public with their high-profile designs for downtown Washington, D.C. Encyclopedias by John Greenlee and Rick

Hans Simon's "praerie" planting at the Berggarten in Hannover, Germany, makes extensive use of North American prairie species. It makes deliberate reference to the historic prairie while integrating European and Asian species that match the aesthetic and are adapted to the urban conditions.

Darke documented the new diversity of grasses and illustrated the potential for integrating them in varied landscapes. By 2004, when Piet Oudolf and the James Corner Field Operations team began designing the High Line's gardens, grasses had won wide acceptance in North America's public and private places. Also by then, the trend in landscape grasses and sedges had shifted from problematic exotics such as *Miscanthus* and *Pennisetum* to North American natives including switchgrass (*Panicum*), bluestems (*Schizachyrium* and *Andropogon*) and prairie dropseed (*Sporobolus*). The High Line's grasses reflect this ecologically informed approach.

Cassian Schmidt's design at Hermannshof garden in Weinheim, Germany, combines North American plants including stiff goldenrod (*Solidago rigida* subsp. *humilis*), yellow coneflower (*Echinacea paradoxa*) and Mexican feather-grass (*Nassella tenuissima*) with balloon flower (*Platycodon grandiflorus*), a blue-flowered native of eastern Asia.

Gardens have a centuries-long association with ruins, and the mood of ruin gardens is typically romantic, nostalgic, contemplative. The majority of European ruins were once homes, churches or battlements. Because the age of industry comprises a much greater portion of U.S. history, ruins there tend to be remnants of factories, mills and railroads. Contemporary North American society has only recently begun to see these as having romantic qualities or as being worthy of contemplation. Indeed, there are now significant subcultures devoted to exploring such places. Urban exploration, aka *UE* or *UrbEx*, has a growing international following. The dystopian landscape and the romantic landscape are no longer antithetical. The landscape of the abandoned High Line—an authentic ruin—was a destination for urban explorers. Recreated as a series of contempletive gardens, the same landscape now safely provides an opportunity for millions to experience the thrill of discovery inherent in places of accidental origin.

Accidental landscapes evolved from derelict (*disused* is the term in Great Britain) railroad rights-of-way are superb places to observe regenerative biological processes. Anyone who doubts the vibrancy of pioneer species in emerging ecologies need only to walk one of these lines. Grasses are among the most capable pioneers. They are ubiquitous in the early stages of reclamation when the landscape tends to be open and sunny, and often form the matrix into which later arrivals establish themselves. As woody pioneers bring shade to the ground layer, grasses eventually give way to trees, and thickets evolve into woodlands.

In this Anthropocene era, when human influence is the principal force shaping the global ecology, regenerative landscapes everywhere usually involve an amalgam of indigenous and introduced species. St. Johns University biologist Richard Stalter's 2004 Torrey Botanical Society article "The Flora on the High Line, New York City, New York"[9] documented 161 plant species growing spontaneously on the wild High Line, with a nearly even mix of 82 indigenous and 79 introduced. The team that designed the High Line's gardens witnessed these patterns and dynamics firsthand and built them into the choreography, plantings and stewardship that distinguish the High Line today. In numerical terms, plant diversity is higher now than ever before, with nearly 400 different species growing on the High Line as of late 2016.

We were all interested in how the site's found state of dereliction might inspire a design language and how the metaphor of the ruin and its association with nostalgia and dystopia might be addressed.[10]
— ELIZABETH DILLER

Top left: Spontaneous growth of native gray birch (*Betula populifolia*) creates woodland thickets along derelict rail lines running through Pennsylvania's coal mining region.

Top right: Pitch pine (*Pinus rigida*) and switchgrass (*Panicum virgatum*) grow on abandoned railroad right-of-way in the New Jersey pine barrens.

Bottom left and right: Grasses mix with broad-leaved perennial and biennial pioneer species on Philadelphia's abandoned Reading Viaduct.

Overleaf: Locally indigenous European birch (*Betula pendula*) grows in thickets in Berlin's Natur-Park Südgelände.

From top, left to right: The unreconstructed High Line from its razor-
wired stage (2002) through the initial
visit of the design team (2004) and

Piet Oudolf's continuing observation
of the site with colleagues Rick Darke
and Dale Hendricks (2006).

Opposite: Landscape architect James
Corner contemplating the High Line's
spontaneous patterns, October
2004.

One of the most powerful impressions when we first stepped onto the High Line was
the effect of nature taking over the ruin. The High Line is a massive steel and concrete structure,
and so the sheer abundance of plants and even birdsong was a real surprise. The inspiration
for the design was right in front of us.[11] — JAMES CORNER

Unique as they are, the High Line's gardens have their precedents. The Bridge of Flowers in Shelburne Falls, Massachusetts, and Paris's Promenade Plantée are early examples of derelict rail landscapes recast as gardens. The similarity ends with the plantings: neither one invites dynamic process into the design. Natur-Park Südgelände in Berlin's Schöneberg-Templehof district is the most relevant precedent. Originally a railyard dating to the 1880s, this 18-hectare park repurposes trackways as pathways and is clothed almost entirely with the spontaneous vegetation that colonized the site after its abandonment in 1952. Studies by the Technical University of Berlin's Institute of Ecology documented 366 plant species growing there by 1992;[12] however, continuing observation has shown a decrease in diversity as woodlands displace herbaceous plant communities. The dilemma is how and when to intervene in spontaneous biological process to conserve diversity. There's a word for such intervention: it's called gardening.

Piet Oudolf's artistic approach to garden design has been increasingly informed by dynamic living processes. In early years he, along with most designers working in a naturalistic style, was still organizing plantings in discrete blocks. The planting blocks were irregular in

Piet Oudolf's first matrix planting in a public garden in the United States, at Chicago's Lurie Garden.

Opposite: Wild grasses form the background matrix with seedheads of redroot (*Lachnanthes tinctoria*) appearing in rhythmic sweeps in this late autumn view of a derelict cranberry bog in the New Jersey pine barrens. These native wildings are dismissed as weeds by cranberry growers.

I look for plants that have another life after living. — PIET OUDOLF

Coauthors Piet Oudolf and Henk Gerritsen first referred to the evocative broad-leaved perennials and grasses they were developing as "dream plants" in their book *Droomplanten* published in the Netherlands in 1990.[13] The dreamy effect possible is evident in this recent winter photo of Piet and Anja Oudolf's garden in Hummelo. Seed stalks stand in a grassy matrix while the shapes of peripheral hedges evoke the form of distant woodlands. The composition is perfect in its imperfection.

shape, varied in size and overlapping each other. Seen from a distance, and especially when viewed from oblique angles, block plantings give an impression of the nuanced intermingling of matrix-based plant communities. However, when viewed up close it becomes clear they're a static oversimplification.

In 2004 Piet experimented with matrix-based design for a section of his plantings in Chicago's Lurie Garden, and the dynamism of this approach was readily apparent and well-received. When Lisa Switkin of James Corner Field Operations soon after invited him to join the High Line design team, Piet decided to adapt matrix design to the High Line on a grand scale. The result is a series of gardens that appear spontaneous and dynamic because, to a great extent, they are. The design ethic is to combine locally adapted, mutually compatible long-lived plants in layered associations that draw from wild communities but don't attempt to replicate them literally. This approach anticipates and encourages some amount of naturalization. It ensures the gardens and their plantings will evolve, incrementally, as the relative strengths of different species shift in response to changing conditions. In multiple ways, the High Line's gardens are following the course of many successional landscapes in the temperate northeast, as shade from trees—or new buildings—drives adaptation.

How are the gardens of the High Line elevating the nature of modern landscapes? They're demonstrating that the worthiest goal is not to reprise yesterday's Nature, or culture, but rather to redefine the character of modern gardens. They offer a character model based on continual observation and reinvention that best serves local, regional and global human and nonhuman communities. As stewards, the Friends of the High Line staff and volunteers have proved equally capable as leaders and listeners. The High Line is contributing to garden craft by mentoring and supporting a new breed of gardeners with unprecedented skills in managing dynamic landscapes.

Despite the responsibility of serving a potentially overwhelming number of visitors, the High Line has not become solemn: it remains seriously playful. Though it's unlikely there will ever be another place quite like the High Line, it offers a wealth of insights and approaches worthy of emulation in gardens large or small, public or private. Authentic in spirit and execution, the High Line's gardens offer a journey that is intriguing, unpredictable, imperfect and, above all, transformative.

Serious design is imperfect. It's filled with the kind of craft laws that come from something being the first of its kind. The art of serious play is about invention, change, rebellion—not perfection.[14]
— PAULA SCHER

The one tool I can't be
without are my eyes.
Sometimes you need a spade,
sometimes pruners,
but when you are gardening
you really have to look.
— PIET OUDOLF

GARDENS OF THE HIGH LINE

RAIL YARDS

12th Avenue

COACH TOWER
10 HUDSON YARDS

WILDFLOWER FIELD
& RADIAL PLANTINGS

10th Avenue

FLYOVER

11th Avenue

MEADOW WALK

23rd STREET LAWN
& SEATING STEPS

CHELSEA THICKET

CHELSEA GRASSLANDS

10th Avenue

HUDSON RIVER

CHELSEA PIERS

10th AVENUE SQUARE

NORTHERN SPUR

CHELSEA
MARKET

HUDSON RIVER
OVERLOOK

SUNDECK & WATER GARDEN

WASHINGTON GRASSLANDS

THE STANDARD

GANSEVOORT WOODLAND

FRIENDS OF THE
HIGH LINE

WHITNEY MUSEUM
OF AMERICAN ART

West 36th Street

West 35th Street

West 34th Street

West 33rd Street

West 32nd Street

Dyer Avenue

West 30th Street

West 29th Street

West 28th Street

West 27th Street

West 26th Street

West 25th Street

West 24th Street

West 23rd Street

West 22nd Street

West 21st Street

West 20th Street

West 19th Street

West 18th Street

West 17th Street

West 16th Street

West 15th Street

West 14th Street

West 13th Street

Little West 12th Street

Gansevoort Street

Greenwich Street

Hudson Street

Horatio Street

West 4th Street

Greenwich Avenue

10th Avenue

11th Avenue

9th Avenue

8th Avenue

7th Avenue

Washington Street

GANSEVOORT WOODLAND

Gansevoort Street to Little West 12th Street

Where does a garden begin? If the design is truly good, the journey can start anywhere. The first impression will be deeply memorable, the initial experience uniquely enjoyable. The High Line is like this—virtually any of its access points opens onto an exhilarating garden. Other gardens, however—especially those whose layout has evolved over time—have no clear starting point, no grand entrance. The High Line isn't like this. Its gardens were designed together as a choreographed experience, and the most dramatic place to begin is at the Gansevoort Street stair.

The team that designed the High Line was led by the landscape architectural firm James Corner Field Operations, with James Corner and Lisa Switkin as principals on the project. When assembling the rest of the team, they knew, as Lisa has recalled, that "the novelty of the project demanded collaborators who were challenging their disciplines within and at the margins."[15] They invited the architectural firm Diller Scofidio + Renfro (DS+R), inspired by the theatrical quality of its work. They asked Piet Oudolf to join because of his unique expertise in evocative, naturalistic plantings. The broad narrative of the High Line's landscape was defined by the landscape architects, and Piet was responsible for the detailed planting designs that would bring it to life.

Together, the team articulated design principles and goals that have proved astonishingly prescient in establishing the unique character of the High Line's gardens. Taking time to reflect on these, as they appear in the initial proposal and in the submitted design,[16] will enrich any visitor's experience of the High Line. A key principle is that the gardens should "remain perpetually unfinished, sustaining emergent growth and change over time." The goals include creating "a distinct identify that draws on the unusual found conditions of the site" and developing "a varied and intimate choreography to encourage visitors to keep a slow pace and allow themselves to be distracted."

The innovative scripting and pacing of the High Line's landscape are powerfully evident in the "slow stair" that introduces visitors to the elevated gardens. Its steps, risers and interim landing are all designed to slow and stretch the journey, encouraging intimate contemplation of the riveted steel structure while heightening the ancipation of a transformative emergence into Gansevoort Woodland.

It was important that visitors could be uniquely exposed to the historical structure as a kind of introduction to the High Line, positioning them directly under and within the depth of its massive beams.[17] — MATTHEW JOHNSON

Redbuds (*Cercis canadensis*), including the cultivated variety 'Appalachian Red', greet visitors entering Gansevoort Woodland in early May.

Gansevoort Woodland is the High Line's southernmost garden area, designed to provide the arrival experience of entering a wooded thicket. It does this beautifully and dynamically. Observant visitors will first be intriqued by dancing patterns projected on the corten steel panels bordering the stair. At the top, closely spaced gray birches (*Betula populifolia*) dominate an authentic woodland experience enlivened by the framing, opacity, translucency and qualities of line and shadowplay that are characteristic of the eastern North American forest ecosystem. Gray birch is Gansevoort Woodland's signature tree, and it is also one of the most powerful signatures of the High Line's gardens. This relatively small, typically multistemmed tree is a pioneer species that is often among the first to colonize sunny disturbed sites including rocky road cuts and abandoned railroad lines. Although individual stems may be short-lived, new sprouts usually replace them, extending the tree's lifespan. Unlike many white-barked birches, gray birch tolerates the hot, dry conditions typical of urban spaces and is resistant to the bronze birch borer.

Selection and sourcing of the High Line's plants are collaborative processes, and Piet Oudolf has always encouraged suggestions from colleagues. River birch (*Betula nigra*) was originally considered for Gansevoort Woodland. Patrick Cullina, an early advisor to the team who later became the High Line's first head of horticulture, suggested gray birch as a more appropriately scaled alternative. The team agreed, and the next step was to find trees. The typical species form of gray birch is rarely cultivated, but Cullina knew of sources for 'Whitespire', a cultivated variety with exceptionally white bark. Most of the High Line's gray birches are of this variety.

Spring shadows cast by Gansevoort
Woodland tree trunks and foliage play
over steel tracks and corten panels.

The layered structure of Gansevoort Woodland contributes to its all-seasons beauty and its functionality. Gray birches form the canopy layer, with dogwoods (*Cornus florida*), redbuds (*Cercis canadensis*) and shadbushes (*Amelanchier*) making up the understory. The shrub layer includes Japanese clethra (*Clethra barbinervis*) and Dawn viburnum (*Viburnum* x*bodnantense* 'Dawn'). The herbaceous layer includes a diverse mix of flowering broad-leaved perennials, bulbs, grasses, sedges and ferns.

The warm glow of early evening sunlight illuminates Gansevoort Woodland in this mid-April view from one of the Whitney Museum terraces. The ever-present urban context ensures the scale of the High Line's gardens is at once intimate and immense. Though Dawn viburnum is barely discernable from this height, its color and fragrance are inescapable delights for visitors passing by.

Overleaf: The view on foot of Gansevoort Woodland layers, taken earlier on the same day as the above.

Among the pleasures of life in a cold temperate climate such as New York's is the anticipation of seasons to follow. Seasonal change occurs in a near-infinite succession of small moments, and learning to see and understand these little happenings is a worthy lifetime pursuit. John Stilgoe refers to this as "visual acuity" in his classic *Outside Lies Magic: Regaining History and Awareness in Everyday Places*. In these two mid-April photos, the swollen flower buds of a Gansevoort Woodland shadbush are about to open. The bud scales that have protected them from winter's dessicating winds are suffused with the ruddy red tones of brick meatpacking buildings along Washington Street.

Close observation reveals shadbush (*Amelanchier* ×*grandiflora*) bud scales echoing the ruddy red tones of brick meatpacking buildings.

Opposite: Each year by late April, Gansevoort Woodland is transformed by the flowering of shadbush trees. The woodland canopy allows most of the available sunlight to reach the ground, enabling the emergence and growth of plants in the herbaceous layer.

From top: The distinct bronze-green emerging leaves of shadbush are visible among clouds of snow-white flowers.

Pennsylvania sedge (*Carex pensylvanica*) blooms in the herbaceous layer.

The diminutive daffodil (*Narcissus* 'Hawera') adds its clear lemon yellow to the mix.

The immersive experience of
Gansevoort Woodland in April.

The yearly flowering times of trees can vary by a week or two depending upon seasonal weather patterns; however, the relative flowering order of different species is usually consistent. Shadbush is always the first to bloom, followed by eastern redbud (*Cercis canadensis*) and flowering dogwood (*Cornus florida*). In cool springs, shadbush flowers last a week or more, but if the weather is especially warm they can go past peak in a few days. The floral displays of redbuds and dogwoods last longer and the two trees share the trait of flowering before their leaves unfurl. Rebuds have two flowering moments; one when blossoms open on the tree and a second when they fall, carpeting the ground with undiminished color.

Redbuds in Gansevoort Woodland include the pink-purple-flowered typical form, the vibrant pink-red variety 'Appalachian Red' and 'Forest Pansy', a selection with leaves that open looking like purple patent leather and turn bronzy green by late summer.

Left and opposite: Appalachian Red redbud.

Right: Fallen redbud blossoms carpet the ground with undiminished color.

Gansevoort Woodland and the
Tiffany & Co. Foundation Overlook
viewed from across Washington Street.

Piet Oudolf's eye is attuned to the structural qualities of plants, both woody and herbaceous, and his designs place greater importance on architectural character and form than on floral color. Eastern North America's native *Cornus florida* is an example of distinctive structure. Though commonly known as flowering dogwood, the tree's showy ivory-white (or pink) petal-like parts are not flowers but modified leaves properly called bracts. These bracts are sturdier and more durable than petals. Much of this dogwood's unique beauty derives from its

sympodial branching pattern. Most woody plants grow by means of terminal buds that produce stem and branch material. Since the terminal buds of flowering dogwood branches produce flowers, branch elongation continues by means of lateral buds. The result when viewed closely is a rising and falling pattern—a sort of lilting effect—that adds a distinctive cadence to the architecture of the branches.

Virginia bluebells (*Mertensia virginica*) add their vibrant blue hues to the Gansevoort Woodland herbaceous layer, joining dogwoods and redbuds in an association that is common to Eastern North American moist woods and alluvial plain forests. The bluebells are true spring ephemerals, flowering and setting seed before the woodland canopy fills in and shades the ground layer. They go dormant by early summer and in this state they're unaffected by summer heat or drought.

The flowering of Virginia bluebells (*Mertensia virginica*) always overlaps that of dogwoods and redbuds.

By mid-June the ground below Gansevoort Woodland trees and shrubs is nearly covered in a continuous mosaic of herbaceous plants. The pink-purple flowering stalks of Hummelo hedgenettle (*Stachys officinalis* 'Hummelo') stand upright even in shade, though the plants bloom more profusely in sunny spots. The lime-green foliage of autumn moor grass (*Sesleria autumnalis*) now plays an important role suppressing weeds and conserving moisture, as does the low-growing bluestar (*Amsonia* 'Blue Ice').

Pink-purple flowers of Hummelo hedge-nettle (*Stachys officinalis* 'Hummelo') brighten the herbaceous layer in June.

Some of the "peel up" benches are set back, offering varied opportunities for enjoying a bit of intimacy. In summer the woodland canopy provides much-needed shade and cooling.

Vines cascading from the eastern edge of Gansevoort Woodland draw the eye upward and strengthen the connection with the street. Japanese hydrangea vine (*Schizophragma hydrangeoides* 'Moonlight') covers itself with flowers in June. Traditional businesses that earned Chelsea the name "meatpacking district" continue operation along Washington Street below the High Line.

The Tiffany & Co. Foundation Overlook, featured here from three different viewpoints, is located at the southern end of Gansevoort Woodland, offering views over Washington and Gansevoort streets. It is open and airy in spring, then comfortably semi-secluded in summer when the canopy is leafy. The now-truncated High Line once continued through the building on the south side of Gansevoort. Changing billboard-sized artworks (*above and below*) are displayed over the former opening.

In late summer the woodland floor is a study in greens. The form and texture of ferns including dwarf lady fern (*Athyrium felix-femina* 'Minutissima') and Christmas fern (*Polystichum acrostichoides*) complement the linearity of sedges including *Carex laxiculmis*.

The steel rails are originals dating to New York Central Railroad's construction of the High Line in the early 1930s. They were reinstalled after repair of the underlying structure, with the wooden ties spaced wider to accommodate plantings.

The Gansevoort Woodland garden is spectacularly transformed in autumn, as plants in all layers contribute to the multicolored display. Shadbush produces every hue from apricot to crimson. Birch and redbud provide a golden backdrop for shadbush and dogwood.

In the herbaceous layer, lavender-blue aromatic aster (*Aster oblongifolius*) tumbles over the tracks while providing essential support for pollinators such as this flower fly.

Aromatic aster (*Aster oblongifolius*, or *Symphyotrichum oblongifolium* according to recent reclassification) occurs naturally in woodlands and prairies over much of the eastern and central United States. Its ability to withstand extremes of winter cold and summer heat make it well-adapted to conditions on the High Line.

Flowering dogwood's fall foliage is lit by afternoon sun streaming across the Hudson River.

Opposite: At lower left below a dogwood, the sturdy stems and seedheads of Hummelo hedgenettle remain upright, adding to the structure and texture of the herbaceous layer.

Autumn color is vibrant even on
this drizzly day in early November.

Gansevoort Woodland birch-lined
tracks mirror the composition
of Berlin's Natur-Park Südgelände
(*see pages 30–31*).

Light-barked gray birches and dark gray multistemmed shadbushes are easily distinguished even when the landscape is snow-covered.

Gansevoort Woodland and the Tiffany & Co. Foundation Overlook in early November. Nighttime in any of the High Line's gardens is uniquely and beautifully provocative.

Say what some poets will, Nature is not so much her own eversweet interpreter, as the mere supplier of that cunning alphabet, whereby selecting and combining as he pleases, each man reads his own peculiar lesson to his own peculiar mind and mood.

— HERMAN MELVILLE

from *Pierre; or, The Ambiguities*, 1852. Melville also authored *Moby Dick*, 1851, and was the grandson of Peter Gansevoort.

WASHINGTON GRASSLANDS

Little West 12th Street to West 14th Street

The transition from Gansevoort Woodland to Washington Grasslands is graceful yet profound. The enveloping woodland canopy feathers out at its northern end, first framing the upcoming space, then easing into the drama of Washington Grasslands' sunny openness. For visitors walking north on the High Line this is the first in a sequence of surprises that occur as the unique character of each garden area is revealed.

Many gardens frame and organize their transitions by introducing structures such as arbors, trellises, walls or buildings. The High Line's gardens benefit from the existing structure of the elevated railway and the infinitely varied architecture of its urban surround. This organizing context is creatively integrated, and much of the gardens' introduced structuring is accomplished with plantings.

Employing the truly organic architecture of plants to define garden spaces is a creative way of increasing ecological functionality. Enclosures, frames and reveals made of plants double as machines for replenishing atmospheric oxygen and sustaining wildlife with food and shelter. Unlike steel, bricks and mortar, the color, form, scent, sound and opacity of organic architecture changes with seasons. The malleability of plantings is equally important, providing less-costly options for adjusting the organization and material character of garden spaces in response to changing context. The High Line's design principles anticipated this need in suggesting that the gardens remain perpetually unfinished and that they sustain changes in plant growth over time.

Since the High Line's initial opening in 2009, Washington Grasslands has already evolved. It was originally conceived as a garden with a grassy signature. Autumn moor grass (*Sesleria autumnalis*) was placed prominently in and around the islandlike area on the south side of The Standard hotel, with purple moor grass (*Molinia caerulea*), prairie June grass (*Koeleria macrantha*) and little bluestem (*Schizachyrium scoparium*) planted in greater numbers to the north. Autumn moor grass has thrived and purple moor grass has persisted, however prairie June grass and little bluestem proved ill-adapted to shade north of the hotel that has increased due to new construction along the east side of the High Line. Responding to change as opportunity, the design of the herbaceous layer has evolved to a less-grassy mix.

The most obvious signature of Washington Grasslands is now Grace smokebush (*Cotinus* 'Grace'), a hybrid between European smokebush (*Cotinus coggygria*) and the southeastern North American native smokebush (*Cotinus obovatus*). Grace smokebush is a subtle presence in early spring, leafing out later than many woody plants, but is an electrifying presence in the sun-lit southern portion in later seasons.

One river birch is visible in the woodland edge as the experience progresses from intimate enclosure to exhilarating expansiveness.

We scripted the experiences we wanted along the line—areas of transition, places to pause and gather, or intimate alcoves.[18]

— LISA SWITKIN

Gansevoort Woodland's layers frame
the emerging view of Washington
Grasslands immediately to the north.

The stature and variety of the High Line's plantings belie the fact that the entire landscape is essentially a green roof. Soil depth ranges from about 9 inches to 48 inches, however the deeper soil is only in a few areas such as the Tiffany & Co. Foundation Overlook or the Flyover, where raised planters are installed or where soil has been mounded up. Typical soil depth is closer to 18 inches. In addition to this limitation, the underlying structure is much like a highway bridge, freezing more quickly and heating up more rapidly than the conventional ground plane. Because these temperature extremes are lethal for many plants normally considered hardy in the New York region, plant selection on the High Line requires constant experimentation and refinement.

The above photo of construction in 2008 illustrates the shallowness of planting beds. Soil depth is only 12–15 inches in this island area just south of The Standard hotel.

Opposite: The new spring green of autumn moor grass and the light yellow of *Narcissus* 'Hawera' brighten the ground layer in the transition from Gansevoort Woodland to Washington Grasslands in April.

Two bluestars are used extensively in Washington Grasslands. Fine-textured threadleaf bluestar (*Amsonia hubrichtii*), an Arkansas native, plays an increased role as an alternative to sun-requiring grasses (*top*). Low-growing *Amsonia* 'Blue Ice' is a durable flowering ground-cover (*bottom*). Both bloom in May and turn gold in fall.

In May, fringetree (*Chionanthus virginicus*) enlivens the shadier area north of The Standard (*top*) followed by goats-beard (*Aruncus* 'Horatio') and astilbes (mostly *Astilbe* 'Visions in Pink') in June (*bottom*).

Hummelo hedgenettle blooms profusely within a lime-green sweep of autumn moor grass in June on the Hudson side of Washington Grasslands.

Compass plant (*Silphium laciniatum*) towers over white stalks of rattlesnake master (*Eryngium yuccifolium*), purple spikes of gayfeather (*Liatris spicata*) and purple coneflower (*Echinacea purpurea*) in July.

The textural richness of the sunny southernmost portion of Washington Grasslands is evident in this July view looking south toward the Whitney Museum of American Art.

Bottom left and opposite: Matt Johnson's *Untitled* (*Swan*) was crafted from one of the High Line's original steel rails in homage to the site's New York Central Railroad history. Its sinuous curves are matched by stems of compass plant.

Top: Compass plant frames the view west across the Hudson to Jersey City and Hoboken.

Bottom right: Purple coneflower attracts and sustains varied wildlife from summer flowering through winter seed dispersal.

Hervé Descottes designed the High Line's lighting to be beautiful, functional and unobtrusive. His superbly realized intent was to keep the lighting below eye level, avoiding glare and preserving the connection with everything above eye level and in the adjacent cityscapes. Thanks to the High Line's narrow walkways, the low down-facing lighting also illuminates low plantings.

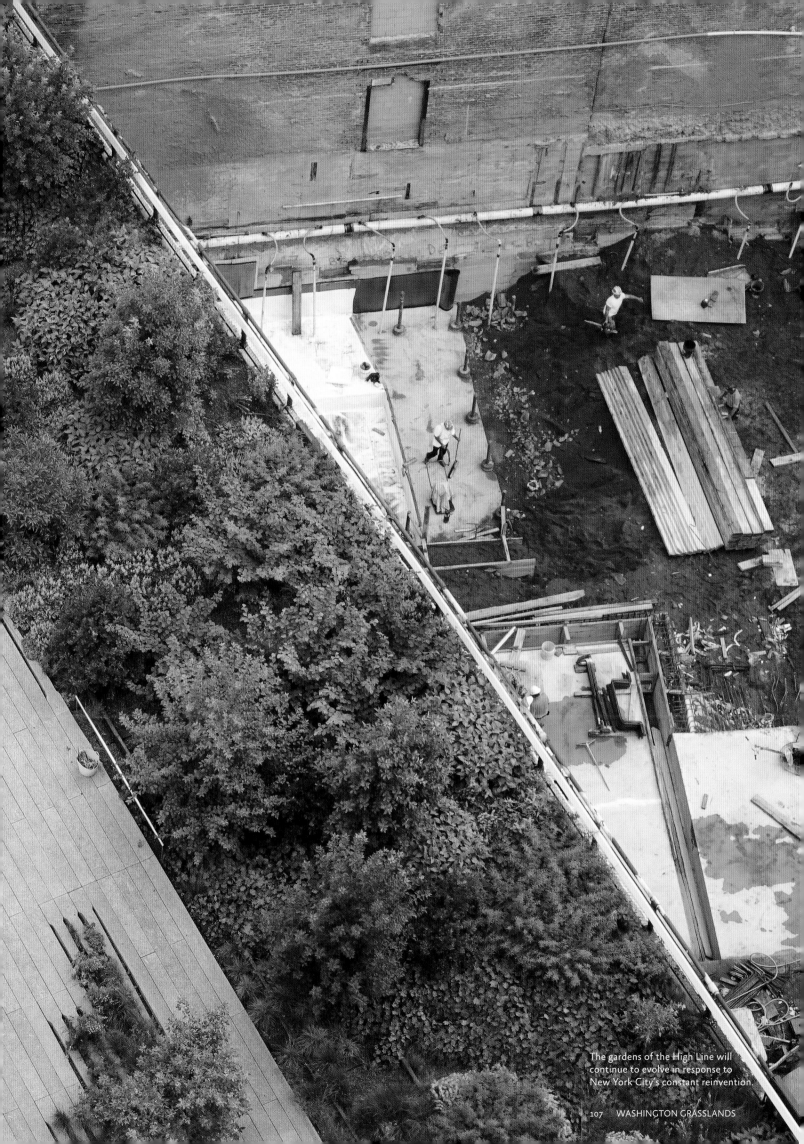

The gardens of the High Line will
continue to evolve in response to
New York City's constant reinvention.

Autumn brings a range of pink and purple hues to Washington Grasslands, including pink muhly grass (*Muhlenbergia capillaris*) (*bottom*), bushclover (*Lespedeza thunbergii* 'Gibraltar') (*top left*), and toadlily (*Tricyrtis* 'Sinonome') (*top right and opposite*).

The layered plantings on the west side north of The Standard include fall-blooming tatarian aster (*Aster tataricus* 'Jindai') and red-spiked mountain fleece (*Persicaria amplexicaulis* 'Firetail').

Meat hooks were once attached to the steel apparatus at upper left, which is preserved in recognition of the High Line's history as supplier to Chelsea's meatpacking district.

Grace smokebush (*Cotinus* 'Grace') combines the best traits of both parents, producing cotton-candy-like flower clusters in early summer followed by spectacular autumn foliage, all on a multistemmed shrub of moderate size. This view and those on the following two pages illustrate the luminous effects of late-day sunlight in June.

The High Line has helped people to rediscover the art of promenading.[19]

—LISA SWITKIN

Early evening sunlight streams
across the Hudson, illuminating and
silhouetting Grace smokebush.

Shaded as it passes under The Standard, this open part of Washington Grasslands is a favored meeting and exhibition space. Kathryn Andrews's sculpture *Sunbathers II* greets visitors, August 2016.

Foliage of *Grace* smokebush nears peak autumn color in early November as threadleaf bluestar carpets the ground. Purple coneflowers stand upright dispersing seeds for visiting birds.

Rashid Johnson's *Blocks* (*at left*) and Frank Stella's *Black Star* (*upper right*) on a Whitney Museum terrace add to the intrigue.

The structure, line and form of the High Line's gardens and plantings are never more beautifully revealed than in winter. A light snow cover accentuates the effect while bringing a rare quiet and calm to the landscape. Friends of the High Line makes every effort to keep the gardens open through winter, and it is a season not to be missed.

HUDSON RIVER OVERLOOK

West 14th Street to West 15th Street, Lower Level

Topography often makes a garden. The natural rise and fall of land add variation to any outdoor experience, with low points providing nestled enclosure and high points offering intriguing views. The High Line's single most distinguishing feature—its elevation above the street—is a topographic one, albeit a constructed one.

It's easy to forget that from a railroad perspective, varied topography is only a threat to efficiency: trains use less energy on level tracks. The High Line's gardens rest on the former rail bed of the New York Central Railroad's West Side Line. When completed in 1934, the gradient of the dual tracks running from 30th Street south past Gansevoort was approximately one percent or less; meaning the grade level changed less than one foot over a distance of 100 feet. The only exception to this was a switchback section of track that split off at 10th Avenue and 14th Street and descended to the level of spurs between 15th and 17th Streets (the northernmost is now the High Line's Northern Spur garden). This switchback created two distinct levels and provided the opportunity to create the Hudson River Overlook and the Sundeck and Water Garden above and to the north of it.

This garden takes advantage of its proximity to the river, offering unique perspectives on historic maritime architecture and activity. Architect Kenneth Murchison's Beaux-Arts styled Hoboken Terminal is the standout on the west bank. Built in 1907 for the Delaware, Lackawanna and Western Railroad, the copper-clad complex was restored to full operation soon after its centennial, connecting New Jersey to Manhattan by ferry and by rails running in tubes under the Hudson. On the east bank the eye is drawn to a steel arch that once framed the entrance to Chelsea Pier 54. Survivors of the *Titanic* were delivered here in 1912. Three years later the *Lusitania* departed for Liverpool and was sunk by torpedoes. The Hudson River Overlook is a superb place to contemplate the river's essential yet conflicted role in shaping the city's landscape and communities.

Views to the west are framed by plantings except for a balcony-like section and an area with peel-up benches toward the southern end. In initial designs this garden was conceived and referred to as a preserve featuring eastern North American native plants. Although the name "preserve" didn't survive, the planting plan did, and today it remains almost exclusively devoted to regionally indigenous species. Various sumacs which have grown to treelike size function as the shrub and canopy layers, with a robust mix of grasses, asters and other tall-growing perennials below.

Viewed from the Hudson River Overlook, the warm light of a mid-July sunset illuminates the rebuilt copper clock tower of Hoboken Terminal on the New Jersey side of the Hudson.

Top and opposite: Sumacs including *Rhus typhina*, *Rhus glabra* and cutleaf forms of these line the Hudson River Overlook for much of its length along 10th Avenue and over 14th Street.

Their fine texture and that of the native grasses and perennials complement the historic steelwork installed at all street crossings.

Bottom: This photo from the New York Central Railroad's *West Side Improvement* booklet [20] looks north from 14th Street, showing the switchback track and dual levels as construction

was nearing completion in 1934. Some of the steel trackwork was saved and embedded in the paved surfaces of the current garden.

Opposite: Refreshingly cool colors welcome summer visitors arriving by the 14th Street stairway. Closely planted little bluestem, mountain mint (*Pycnanthemum muticum*), Joe-Pye-weed (*Eupatorium*) and blazing star (*Liatris*) keep the ground below the cutleaf sumacs covered, conserving moisture and suppressing weeds.

Above: By autumn the stairway planting has shifted to warm tones, backing the vibrant lavender-blue of aromatic aster.

The open western exposure closely ties the look of this landscape to the character of sunlight. Colors that appear especially saturated on a dim, overcast autumn day (*top*) are equally enhanced when backlit by the low-angled late day light of a clear day (*bottom*).

Top: Sunset over the Hudson is a memorable event at any time of year when observed from the Hudson River Overlook. The steel arch surviving from former Cunard Lines Pier 54 is a reminder of Manhattan's continually evolving relationship with the river.

Below: Another example of how the brilliant subtlety of the low, down-facing lighting illuminates the walkway and plantings without diminishing the visual allure of the adjacent nightscape.

SUNDECK & WATER GARDEN

West 14th Street to West 15th Street, Upper Level

Positioned on the main level above the Hudson River Overlook, this space is also beautifully sunlit from midday to sunset. The Sundeck's wooden benches invite visitors to kick back and take a break from the journey north or south. Some of these are moveable, having flanged steel wheels that ride on rails, like train cars. An overarching canopy of sumacs is underplanted with a fine-textured mix of grasses and threadleaf bluestar enveloping the benches in a soft surround. In warm months the benches are almost continually occupied, and this is one of the most popular places to watch and be watched. By late autumn, crowds have thinned and it's easy to relax in relative quiet with a book, an apple, or a friend. The benches face west to the Water Garden, which awakens slowly in spring but hits its stride by early summer and remains vibrant and colorful into winter.

Although one of the more fantastic plans submitted to the preliminary design competition imagined the High Line's landscape as one long lap pool, the reality is that any conventional sort of water garden would be impractical atop such an elevated and exposed site. Yet water is a uniquely sensual presence in gardens: wonderful to touch, watch, listen to, and often longed for in its absence. This garden represents an elegant design solution that makes water and the enjoyment of it a distinctly memorable and sustainable part of the overall experience. The space presents opportunities to interact with moving water or to simply be by it, engaged in thought or conversation. The core feature is a scrim fountain that sends a thin sheet of water rippling across pavement that is sloped so gently as to be imperceptible. A subtle drain along the edge collects the water for recirculation. Peel-up benches within the scrim encourage barefoot adventures, though the water is so shallow it can be traversed in street shoes.

In natural systems, the presence or absence of water profoundly influences the makeup of associated plant and animal communities. The Water Garden tells this ecological story with style and authenticity by lining the edges of the scrim fountain with an association of plant species typical of New York area wetland communities. Regionally native species include swamp milkweed (*Asclepias incarnata*), cardinal flower (*Lobelia cardinalis*), bitter panicgrass (*Panicum amarum*), white turtlehead (*Chelone glabra*), Joe-pye-weed (*Eupatorium*) and swamp rose-mallow (*Hibiscus moscheutos*). Coexisting with these are graceful cattail (*Typha laxmannii*) and dwarf cattail (*Typha minima*), both Eurasian natives that resemble but are smaller and less aggressive than the North American common cattail (*Typha latifolia*).

Totems by artist Mariana Castillo Deball are complemented by the early November colors of sumacs and other sundeck plantings in this view to the north.

Dappled light adds character to the September landscape, illuminating and highlighting Dewey Blue bitter panicgrass (*Panicum amarum* 'Dewey Blue'), cardinal flower and (*opposite*) Korean feather-reed grass (*Calamagrostis brachytricha*).

The Sundeck and its water garden together are one of the most interactive and social spaces on the High Line. In warm months the scrim fountain invites play while reflecting colors of the summer sky. The virtual wall of wetland plants creates a sense of intimacy and enclosure.

Above: Viewed from the lower level, the Water Garden's community of wetland species is dramatically different from the dryland species along the left edge of the walkway. In this mid-August photo, swamp rose-mallow opens new pink flowers while seed-pods of earlier blooms mature and turn brown. Cattails tower over swamp milkweed and Joe-Pye-weed has finished blooming and is developing its seeds.

Opposite, from left: Swamp rose-mallow; seedpods of swamp rose-mallow.

Bottom right: Swamp milkweed flowers.

A newly emerged monarch butterfly seeks nectar from swamp milkweeds in mid-August. This migratory butterfly is doubly sustained by these plants, since milkweed leaves are the sole food of monarchs in larval (caterpillar) stage.

Harvest colors enveloping the Sundeck's benches set the tone for quiet enjoyment of an apple and a book as autumn temperatures dip.

Passing by the benches in a snowstorm is reminiscent of the beach in winter. There's a solitary beauty in the quiet, reflecting on a past summer's conversations and anticipating those to come.

NORTHERN SPUR

West 16th Street

Experienced gardeners know that some of the most distinctive designs result from challenges that at first seem daunting. That's the story of the Northern Spur. Completed by 1934, the Spur created a connection to the Merchants Refrigerating Company warehouse. Unlike many buildings constructed in concert with the West Side Line, this vast, pre-existing cold storage facility was retrofitted to take advantage of rail delivery of meats and produce.

Suspended over 10th Avenue, the Spur presented a visually dramatic opportunity for planting. Horticulturally, it is an especially difficult space, with growing conditions impacted by shallow planting depth, heat reflected from the pavement below and freezing and thawing that is amplified due to the thinness and exposure of the structure. Since no walkway was planned, access for subsequent care would also be challenging, and this provided additional motivation to create a planting palette with exceptional vigor and durability.

The solution, which has proved highly successful from both aesthetic and practical viewpoints, was to restrict the design to the toughest, most resilient species. More than a decade has passed since the initial planting, and survivorship has been astonishing. North American natives dominate the mix, though this is an unintentional result of the focus on hardiness. Among these, skyblue aster (*Aster azureus*), Pennsylvania sedge (*Carex pensylvanica*), wild-oat (*Chasmanthium latifolium*), Indian physic (*Porteranthus stipulatus*), wild spurge (*Euphorbia corollata*), wild geranium (*Geranium maculatum*), wild stonecrop (*Sedum ternatum*), white snakeroot (*Eupatorium rugosum*), boneset (*Eupatorium perfoliatum*), hairy alumroot (*Heuchera macrorhiza* 'Autumn Bride'), bluestem goldenrod (*Solidago caesia*) and foamflower (*Tiarella cordifolia*) continue to thrive. One of the relatively few non-natives in the original mix, Siberian catmint (*Nepeta sibirica*), has not persisted on the Spur though it has in other areas. Cold-hardiness isn't the issue, since this species was introduced from Siberian and northern Chinese mountain habitats over 8000 feet in elevation. Though cold, these steep places are sunny and sharply drained. New York City's relatively overcast and soggy winter conditions, intensified by the Spur, may be the culprit.

When the warehouse building was converted to offices in the early 1980s, the entry point of the tracks was sealed with bricks. Observant visitors will notice the telltale variation in color and pattern of the newer masonry. This and innumerable other changes encountered along the High Line are reminders that the landscape is like a palimpsest—a surface written on repeatedly, each previous writing having been imperfectly erased and remaining partly legible. At one point shrubs were placed at the end of the Spur, obscuring the bricked-over entrance, but they've since been removed. The question of why a railroad would head into a brick wall is an indelible intrigue of this garden.

Plantings comprised mostly of North American natives near their autumn color peak in mid-October as the Northern Spur crosses 10th Avenue.

Growing conditions on the Northern
Spur are hot and dry in summer and
cold and wet in winter.

Hot town, summer in the city as the Northern Spur bakes over 10th Avenue in mid-July.

As a result of the focus on North American natives, especially eastern woodland species, the Northern Spur has a flush of bloom in spring, is relatively green and leafy in summer, and is at its flower and foliage color peak in autumn. Late winter and early spring are its least colorful periods. About a year after the initial planting, minor bulbs including lesser glory-of-the-snow (*Chionodoxa sardensis*) and Persian squill (*Scilla mischtschenkoana*) were planted to enhance early season interest. Adapted to the hot, dry summers and cold, wet winters typical of the Mediterranean climate of their native Caucasus, these and other minor bulbs from similar regions are superbly suited to conditions commonly encountered in urban gardens.

Light blue-flowered *Scilla mischtschenkoana* and dark blue-flowered *Chionodoxa sardensis* enliven the Northern Spur landscape in March and April. Pennsylvania sedge is the sole North American native blooming along with them.

Opposite: Seeds and insects living in organic matter at ground level provide sustenance for avian wildlife including native and introduced sparrows.

Truly sustainable gardening is devoted to preserving resources. Since modifications to growing conditions including soil makeup, fertility, drainage and hydrology all use resources, the least consumptive approach is to adapt plants to place rather than adapt place to plants. This may mean that a particular plant, such as Siberian catmint, isn't sustainable in a given place, no matter how desirable it may be.

High Line horticulture is a continual experiment dedicated to determining the most beautiful and appropriate plants and plant associations for each of the varied garden habitats. This approach ensures the gardens will be a living model of responsible gardening.

Opposite: Siberian catmint was dramatic in the first couple of years after the initial planting but proved ill-adapted to conditions. Rather than replant continually, it was allowed to fade from the mix.

Top, from left: Wild geranium with hairy alumroot; wild stonecrop with pink wood sorrel (*Oxalis debilis*) and wild-oat.

Bottom left and right: Indian physic foliage and flowers

Indian physic adds its delicate white
flowers to a richly textured study in
greens in mid-June.

The foliage of many herbaceous perennials becomes yellow or gold in fall but red is an uncommon color. Indian physic is a dramatic exception, reliably turning crimson in October and November.

Colorful flowers of skyblue aster and bluestem goldenrod are complemented by fluffy seedheads of *Eupatorium* species in autumn.

Juxtaposition with 10th Avenue's often frenetic activity adds to the drama of the Northern Spur.

Red highlights in the suspended seed-heads of wild-oat match the foliage of Indian physic in this late-September view.

10th AVENUE SQUARE

West 16th Street to West 18th Street

The High Line's dynamic and richly layered landscape presents infinite opportunities to practice the art of observation. The complexity of its plantings and the diversity of its visitors ensure life on the Line is endlessly intriguing. Though the planning process deliberately scripted a myriad of experiential opportunities, unscripted response has always been the design goal. Inspired by a spontaneous garden populated by truly autonomous wildlings, this reimagined landscape remains a genuinely wild place.

When speaking at the University of Lille in 1854, scientist Louis Pasteur suggested, "In the field of observation, chance favors only the prepared mind." The 10th Avenue Square with its brilliantly resourceful overlook proves this concept. Because gardens are great staging grounds for storytelling, open-air theaters have often been included in their makeup. The West Side Line's 10th Avenue crossing stood for three-quarters of a century before anyone imagined it as a theater. It took the design team's prepared minds to recognize a unique chance to create a signature element. The finished theater's perspective on the bustling avenue below is mesmerizing, day or night. The view north to the Coach tower, a dozen blocks away at Hudson Yards, offers insight and orientation to Chelsea distances. At street level or from the eastern edge of Chelsea Grasslands, the view to the theater is proof of why this place is so captivating.

Adjacent to the overlook theater, the Square offers a place to meet or relax under an ordered grove of trifoliate maples (*Acer triflorum*). Native to northeastern China and Korea, this relatively small maple is prized for its heat tolerance, brassy exfoliating bark and vibrant orange-red autumn color. Its spreading canopy is leafy enough to cool the space but open enough to allow pleasingly dappled light to reach the ground layer. Seating and walking surfaces below the maples and in the theater are constructed of ipe (*Handroanthus*), the walnut-like wood of a commercially farmed tropical American tree. On clear days it's possible to look south from the maple grove, over the Northern Spur to the Statue of Liberty and Ellis Island.

The majority of this busy square's plantings are organized along its edges. Grace smoke-bush is a distinctive presence in an island separating the main level from the walkway to the Northern Spur. Purple milkweed (*Asclepias purpurascens*) is a standout in the herbaceous layer when in bloom and again when its rocketship-shaped seedpods mature.

Like many of the designs, the 10th Avenue overlook took advantage of what was already there. It's a mini theater for a simple urban drama. It's startling from the street when you look up and suddenly realize you have an audience, and in this case, the audience is also on stage.[21]
— MATTHEW JOHNSON

Looking north over 10th Avenue
in mid-August.

The 10th Avenue Square's trifoliate maple grove after a midsummer cloudburst.

Despite its wide native range in central, southern and eastern North America, purple milkweed (*Asclepias purpurascens*) is relatively uncommon in cultivation. The June flowers (*above*) develop into rocketship-shaped seedpods by October (*opposite*).

BEYOND
THIS POINT
YOU MAY
ENCOUNTER
NUDE
SUNBATHERS

Another example of a gracefully scripted transitional experience, as the treed enclosure of the Square opens on the luminous landscape of Chelsea Grasslands.

CHELSEA GRASSLANDS

West 18th Street to West 20th Street

Grasses have always been essential to the High Line and always will be. Pioneers in the ecological sense, they were among the first living things to find opportunity in the derelict West Side Line's emerging habitat. Aesthetically, they're key to the pioneering urban naturalism that distinguishes the re-imagined landscape. Unlike their close relatives the sedges, most true grasses are sun plants, so it is fitting that Chelsea Grasslands, one of the sunniest spaces on the 'Line, is where they reach the zenith of their drama and diversity.

Changelings by nature, grasses contribute more to the gardens' dynamic character than any other plant group. Their colors, though less saturated than typical flowering plants, are softly sophisticated and remarkably varied. Color diversity in grasses begins with greens, expressed in every imaginable hue, tint and shade. In autumn, green grasses turn gold, apricot, red and russet in a slow fade to fawn, while blue-green grasses become suffused with silver and purple. Grasses' capacity for self-seeding ensures their patterns are ever in flux and inclines them to grow in large masses. Beyond color, grasses contribute a wealth of beauty and intrigue derived from unique qualities of line, form, texture and translucency. Their lissome stalks and flowers flutter and dance to every summer breeze, autumn storm and winter wind. As they move they sing in low tones ranging from a whisper to a staccato rattle. Grasses' fineness provides beautiful contrast to the bold texture of broad-leaved plants, and their lightness makes them ideal companions to the opacity and fixed forms of art and architecture.

Big bluestem (*Andropogon gerardii*), Indian grass (*Sorghastrum nutans*) and switchgrass (*Panicum virgatum*) are primarily responsible for the grassy splendor of Chelsea Grasslands. Along with little bluestem (*Schizachyrium scoparium*) they are the dominant species of the North American tallgrass prairie, however all are also native to the east, including the New York region. Physiologically, they are warm-season types, and warm-season grasses like it hot, growing best when air temperatures exceed eighty degrees Fahrenheit. They're slow to start in spring and have little height or presence until late May or June. By late summer they've achieved their full stature and mass, radically transforming the entire scale of the landscape.

Lower-growing than its tallgrass prairie companions, little bluestem is least adapted to growing in close proximity to broad-leaved species, especially in densely planted combinations. Though little bluestem is represented in Chelsea Grasslands, the lower tier of grasses is mostly comprised of North American native prairie dropseed (*Sporobolus heterolepis*) and southern European native autumn moor grass (*Sesleria autumnalis*), both of which have proved capable of thriving in the intricate mix.

Chartreuse autumn moor grass occupies the lower tier, as Shenandoah switchgrass (*Panicum virgatum* 'Shenandoah') turns wine-red in early autumn.

Steel rails and the flowers and seed-heads of broad-leaved herbaceous perennial plants beautifully contrast with the fine line and texture of the predominantly grassy mix.

Opposite: Big bluestem (*foreground*) stands over six feet tall in late October. Along with tall-growing companions switchgrass and Indian grass, its presence is as dramatic as any shrub.

Choosing colorful flowering companions to grasses is an art in itself. Though grassy growth is relatively low in spring, it is a potentially overwhelming force in summer and autumn. To survive, plants must take advantage of available light at ground level early in the year, then have strategies for tolerating the shade and competition of grasses in later seasons. Some, such as irises and prairie dock (*Silphium terebinthinaceum*), persist by means of strong, often deep root systems. Others, such as asters, grow tall along with the grasses, flowering in late summer and fall. Many bulbs, including daffodils, species tulips, crocuses, grape hyacinths (*Muscari*), squill (*Scilla*), onions (*Allium*) and snowdrops (*Galanthus*), go dormant after they flower and set seed and are unaffected by the lack of summer sunlight. Chelsea Grasslands' design carefully matches grasses and companions to create a sustainable all-seasons landscape.

Opposite: Copper iris (*Iris fulva*) colorfully enlivens the late-May landscape while grasses are still low. It withstands competition as grasses grow tall.

Above, clockwise from top left: Lady Jane tulip (*Tulipa clusiana* 'Lady Jane'), pheasant's-eye daffodil (*Narcissus poeticus*), Valerie Finnis grape hyacinth (*Muscari armeniacum* 'Valerie Finnis') and early crocus (*Crocus tommasinianus*) bloom in April and May, then go dormant.

Evoking the abandoned Trans-Arabian Pipeline, Rayyane Tabet's *Steel Rings* is dramatically exposed in mid-April, before warm-season grasses begin their new growth.

By mid-July of the same year tall-growing grasses and flowering companions including Culver's root (*Veronicastrum virginicum*) have transformed the landscape. *Steel Rings* is now a subtle presence and the steel railroad tracks below it are nearly obscured.

Woody plants—trees and shrubs—play minor roles in Chelsea Grasslands with the notable exception of a few burr oaks (*Quercus macrocarpa*). This North American native tree frequently occurs with grasses from the Atlantic to the Great Plains. The oaks' inclusion is one of the High Line's many experiments, and to date they are thriving despite limited rooting space. The ground below them is covered by a dense, weed-suppressing mix of grasses and colorful flowering plants including meadow sages (*Salvia pratensis* cultivars 'Rhapsody in Blue' and 'Pink Delight'), which sustain themselves in part by self-sowing. Light yellow twisted-leaf onion (*Allium obliquum*) blooms with them in May.

Above and opposite: Meadow sages (*Salvia pratensis* cultivars 'Rhapsody in Blue' and 'Pink Delight') bloom in May along with twisted-leaf onion, a Eurasian species cultivated for its edible bulbs and flower buds as well as its clear yellow flowers and seedheads.

Below and opposite: Though twisted-leaf onion appears delicate, it is a surprisingly durable element in the landscape. Through much of May and June its light lemon-yellow color complements the blooms of multiple companions including deep red-flowered pincushion plant (*Knautia macedonica*), a European native, and wild quinine (*Parthenium integrifolium*), a white-flowered North American native. When flowering, the onion is alive with bees seeking nectar and pollen.

The tubular flowers of coral honeysuckle (*Lonicera sempervirens*) are favorites of hummingbirds and butterflies. Although the foliage of this North American species is susceptible to mildew, the cultivated variety grown on the High Line, 'Major Wheeler', is virtually mildew-free.

Major Wheeler coral honeysuckle blooms profusely on a trellis that backs benches at the south end of Chelsea Grasslands. The dense growth of this native has proved a favorite perch and singing spot for mockingbirds.

Opposite bottom: Gray birches gracefully separate the benches from the main walk, adding to the sense of intimacy. Late-day sunlight illuminates the red-tinged foliage of Brownies hairy alumroot (*Heuchera villosa* 'Brownies') in this mid-July scene.

This simple but brilliantly balanced combination of Mount Everest Persian onion (*Allium stipitatum* 'Mount Everest') and Visions in Pink Chinese astilbe (*Astilbe chinensis* 'Visions in Pink') demonstrates that qualities of texture and form can be more visually powerful than flowers or color alone. In this mid-June scene the onion's white flowers have become green globes as seeds begin to mature.

Opposite and below: Chelsea Grasslands' floral display hits one of its summer peaks by mid-July, when purple coneflower, Culver's root, Claire Grace wild bergamot (*Monarda fistulosa* 'Claire Grace') and sweet coneflower (*Rudbeckia subtomentosa*) add their forms and colors to the mix.

Early morning light in mid-July creates unique patterns of illumination and shadowplay. The translucency of the grassy matrix below the oaks is dramatically apparent, while sunlight accentuates the lavender-purple spikes of blazing star (*Liatris spicata*) and the ivory-white flower clusters of rattlesnake master (*Eryngium yuccifolium*).

In July, blazing star and rattlesnake master are still taller than many of the grasses.

Opposite: By late autumn, flower spikes of the blazing star have turned to tawny seedheads.

This house sparrow is one of many birds, both introduced and native, that find sustenance in the maturing seeds of grasses such as prairie dropseed.

Unusual among grasses, prairie dropseed flowers are powerfully fragrant. The scent has been likened to crushed cilantro or burnt buttered popcorn.

Black lace elderberry (*Sambucus nigra* 'Eva') provides color and textural contrast within a ground cover of autumn moor grass.

Little bluestem takes on purple tones in early autumn. In the High Line's original design the cultivated variety 'The Blues' was planted exclusively, however it is being systematically replaced with 'Standing Ovation', a more upright and adaptable selection shown here.

Many of the most artful compositions are at their best after flowers have gone to seed, as illustrated by this mix of prairie dropseed, compass plant (*Silphium laciniatum*) and purple prairie clover (*Dalea purpurea*).

The fanlike form of purple prairie clover (*foreground*) contributes to this mix with Visions in Pink astilbe, Mount Everest Persian onion, prairie dropseed and Joe-Pye-weed (*Eupatorium dubium*).

By mid-July the tiny capsules of Mount Everest Persian onion have opened to display coal-black seeds.

In October and early November the brilliant gold color of threadleaf bluestar sets off aromatic aster and Shenandoah switchgrass.

The structural beauty of seed stalks and fading foliage becomes ever more evident as late autumn approaches.

The burr oaks join in the late-autumn
color shift to red-orange and apricot,
dark gold and deep brown.

Nearly five months after its yellow
flowers brightened the summer scene,
twisted-leaf onion's sinuous stalks
and silver-brown seedpods are
captivating elements of the late-
autumn landscape.

The texture and color of an historic tenement building at the southern edge of Chelsea Grasslands are complemented by a sea of sturdy stalks and seedheads.

Bent under the weight of maturing seedheads, stalks of prairie dock are set off by the still-upright linearity of big bluestem in early autumn.

The shocking pink flowers of Visions in Pink astilbe have morphed into red-brown seedheads by late September, providing an entirely different color contrast with prairie dropseed, compass plant, Missouri coneflower, and purple-flowered New York ironweed (*Vernonia noveboracensis*).

Dry leaves of prairie dock take on uniquely sculptural qualities by late autumn and persist through winter.

A study in browns enlivens the late-November landscape.

Long after flowers have faded, the structural qualities of plants carry the landscape. Here and opposite, Visions in Pink astilbe, compass plant and Joe-pye-weed are set off by snow and night lighting in early March.

The uniquely grassy character of Chelsea Grasslands segues gracefully at its northern edge into the shrubs and trees that mark the beginning of Chelsea Thicket. Deliberate yet delicate choreography of such transitions is what energizes journeys through the gardens of the High Line in all seasons.

Cutback

The cutback is the single most significant annual event in the life cycle of the High Line's gardens. It's laudable for the ways in which it is done, but the most admirable aspect is its timing. Contrary to the long-established horticultural custom of "putting the garden to bed for winter," the High Line delays the cutback of herbaceous plants until March, and the horticultural, ecological and aesthetic benefits of this approach are profound.

When allowed to remain, dry foliage from the previous year's growth helps protect plants from the dessicating and freezing effects of winter winds. It also offers shelter for wildlife including birds, hibernating butterflies and other beneficial insects. Stalks standing through winter provide perches for avian life and are necessary for the effective wind dispersal of seeds. Looking beyond mere functionality, the lines, forms, textures and patterns of last season's dried life contribute a world of beauty to the winter landscape that is readily accessible to anyone taking the time to observe closely.

Why cutback at all? One simple reason is to minimize the amount of debris on walks and in seating areas in spring, when partly decomposed stems and leaves are most likely to be scattered by the wind. A more complex but no less important motive is to manage plants' long-term health and the artful balance of the overall planting design. No one cuts back plants in wild habitats, however the density and species diversities of the High Line are higher per square yard than that of many temperate northeastern North American habitats. Cutting back is a necessary management tool in the preservation of this diversity. When plants are cut back low to the ground, gardeners are better able to assess their heath and vigor. Many herbaceous perennials, including grasses, eventually tend to die out at their centers. Trimming reveals this and signals the need to renew plants by dividing and replanting the healthy outer growth. Cutting back also reveals patterns of self-seeding, making it easier to decide when to intervene in order to preserve the desired compositional balance of the design.

The cutback is done by hand by a hardy mix of staff and volunteers, and the organic harvest resulting from the cutting of over 100,000 plants is then chipped and composted to produce mulch, soil amendment and compost tea to nurture future growth. At one time the raw material was trucked to Fresh Kills landfill on Staten Island for processing, but since 2016 all work is done on site in the High Line's own facilities. The adoption of this self-contained approach to managing its gardens' ecosystem is living proof of the High Line's commitment to responsible stewardhip.

Graceful stalks of Indian physic
(*Porteranthus stipulatus*) and wild-oat
(*Chasmanthium latifolium*) continue
to disperse seeds after bowing to a
February snowstorm. Photo by
Annik La Farge.

A virtual community of volunteers helps High Line staff members cut back over 100,000 plants in March, just in time before the first stirrings of spring growth. Photo by Annik La Farge.

Opposite: For both safety and practicality, the cutback is done with hand tools held by carefully gloved hands. The harvested organic matter is gathered in large bags for chipping, composting and compost-tea making in the High Line's on-site facilities. Photo by Annik La Farge.

Daffodils are among many early-blooming bulbs that brighten the landscape with their flowers soon after the cutback. Photo by Annik La Farge.

Opposite: The High Line's seasoned staff is trained to recognize many indicators of plant health that are revealed by the newly trimmed landscape. Some plants may need renewal by division. Self-seeding tendencies of others may require encouragement or control. The cutback is an essential tool for preserving the vigor of the High Line ecosystem and the integrity of its design. Photo by Annik La Farge.

CHELSEA THICKET

West 20th Street to West 22nd Street

The transition from Chelsea Grasslands' sunny openness to the wooded environment of Chelsea Thicket is gently paced. It begins slowly, building on the tree and shrub layers and eventually enveloping visitors in the intimacy of a tunnel-like passage. The Thicket's sense of enclosure is heightened by evergreen trees including American holly (*Ilex opaca* cultivars 'Dan Fenton' and 'Jersey Night') and Emerald Sentinel red cedar (*Juniperus virginiana* 'Corcorcor'). Deciduous trees forming the canopy layer include redbuds, sassafras (*Sassafras albidum*), Aurora hybrid dogwood (*Cornus* 'Rutban'), shadbush and gray birch. Though this distinctive, light-barked birch is the signature tree of both Gansevoort Woodland and Chelsea Thicket, dramatic differences in the composition of the shrub and herbaceous layers are responsible for the unique natures of the two wooded gardens.

Fragrance is a key character of the Thicket's shrub layer. Dawn viburnum (*Viburnum xbodnantense* 'Dawn'), winter hazel (*Corylopsis spicata*), Mt. Airy fothergilla (*Fothergilla xintermedia* 'Mt. Airy'), cutleaf lilac (*Syringa xlaciniata*), red-leaf rose (*Rosa glauca*) and Jelena hybrid witchhazel (*Hamamelis xintermedia* 'Jelena') produce a succession of sweetly scented flowers from late winter through spring. In addition to these, a wealth of nonfragrant but still showy shrubs including flowering quinces (*Chaenomeles xsuperba* 'Jet Trail' and *Chaenomeles speciosa* 'Toyo-Nishiki'), winterberry holly (*Ilex verticillata* cultivars 'Red Sprite' and 'Southern Gentleman') and Viking black chokeberry (*Aronia melanocarpa* 'Viking') contribute to the Thicket's unsurpassed floral and fruiting display.

Covering the ground with a living carpet of herbaceous plants rather than mulch is the best way to create all-seasons visual interest while minimizing year-round weeding chores. This is the planting strategy in Chelsea Thicket, and it has been implemented with a mix that is both diverse and unique. The low ground-covering role played by autumn moor grass and prairie dropseed in Chelsea Grasslands is assumed by equally sturdy North American sedges including bromelike sedge (*Carex bromoides*), bristleleaf sedge (*Carex eburnea*) and Bunny Blue sedge (*Carex laxiculmis* 'Hobb'), sometimes in combination with Japanese native Hakone grass (*Hakonechloa macra*). Showy flowering species interspersed with these include European native spring vetch (*Lathyrus vernus*) and Eurasian fumewort (*Corydalis solida*).

Chelsea Thicket is a beautiful illustration of how varying the composition of one or more layers can create a dramatically different landscape mood and experience. Wild habitats can provide similar insights. The canopy of a woodland may continue unchanged for a stretch while the species makeup of lower layers shifts, or the herbaceous layer may be continuous as the diversity of middle or upper layers morphs. The most essential skill to possess, whether designing or conserving layered landscapes, is the ability to observe and articulate the patterns.

The northern edge of Chelsea Thicket
is carpeted with woodland phlox
(*Phlox divaricata*) and foamflowers
(*Tiarella cordifolia* and *Tiarella wherryi*).

The bare, sinuous stems of winter hazel (*Corylopsis spicata*) are hung with fragrant flower spikes in these mid-April images. In mild years this Japanese native sometimes blooms as early as February. The pendent blossoms are followed by delicately pleated leaves that turn rich golden yellow in autumn.

The sweet scent of Dawn viburnum
(*Viburnum xbodnantense* 'Dawn') attracts
visitors and nectar-seeking bees in
April. The building in background is the
Church of the Guardian Angel, built in
1931 along with the High Line.

Opposite: The new growth of brome-like sedge (*Carex bromoides*), bristleleaf sedge (*Carex eburnea*), spring vetch and Frosted Violet coral bells (*Heuchera* 'Frosted Violet') begins to cover the ground layer in April.

Although spring vetch (*Lathyrus vernus*) is uncommon in cultivation, this long-lived European is well suited to North American woodland gardens. It often blooms for weeks in April and May.

Clockwise from top left: Eurasian fume-wort (*Corydalis solida*) blooms under gray birch and with the new leaves of wild ginger (*Asarum canadense*) in April.

Red-leaf rose (*Rosa glauca*) flowers in May, as does cutleaf lilac (*Syringa* x*laciniata*).

Opposite: Mt. Airy fothergilla (*Fothergilla* x*intermedia* 'Mt. Airy') and redbud bloom together in April.

Bunny Blue sedge (*Carex laxiculmis* 'Hobb'), Japanese native Hakone grass (*Hakonechloa macra*) and foamflower beautifully cover the ground while suppressing weeds.

Berries of winterberry holly
(*Ilex verticillata*) brighten the fall
and winter shrub layer.

Flowers of Jelena witchhazel (*Hamamelis xintermedia* 'Jelena') are undaunted by a March snowstorm. This hybrid of Japanese witchhazel (*Hamamelis japonica*) and Chinese witchhazel (*Hamamelis mollis*) often has spectacular red and orange autumn color.

Stems of bloodtwig dogwood (*Cornus sanguinea* 'Midwinter Fire') offer color contrast with gray birches and hollies as giant snowflakes fall on the first day of March. Photo by Annik La Farge.

23rd STREET LAWN & SEATING STEPS

West 22nd Street to West 23rd Street

The Lawn is one of the High Line's great contradictions. It's the antithesis of the naturalism and functional biodiversity that exemplify the High Line's other garden spaces, yet it is literally loved to death—repeatedly.

The Lawn and its associated Seating Steps were designed as meeting and gathering places for friends and strangers and in this they succeed beyond expectations. In their own ways they've assumed a mantle similar to Grand Central Terminal's iconic timepiece, which more than a century ago introduced the phrase, "Meet me under the clock," to New York City's popular culture. The Lawn and Steps are easy to find, natural places to connect.

The trend in contemporary global culture is to view the Lawn as an example of indefensibly conspicuous consumption that is ecologically harmful. When lawns are dependent on irrigation, fertilization and poisons in the form of pesticides and herbicides, this view is fully justified (translated from the Latin, –*cide* means "killer"). Large lawns that go unused and serve only as exercises in control and territoriality are especially hard to defend. Lawns, however, are neither created nor cared for equally. If all residential lawns were reduced to the size of the High Line's and managed with similar conscientiousness, it would be a great gift to the planet.

Readers interested in the origins of the lawn will find Kenneth Jackson's *Crabgrass Frontier: The Suburbanization of the United States* and John Stilgoe's *Borderland: Origins of the American Suburb, 1820–1939* illuminating and entertaining. Though made possible by the machinery of the Industrial Revolution, the lawn was inspired by anti-urbanism. As both books make clear, the birth of the private, residential lawn coincided with the nineteenth-century exodus from the city that was propelled by fear of unhealthy urban conditions. The lawn grew popular along with an increasingly lyrical view of nature. As Jackson writes, it "helped civilize the wild vista beyond and provided a carpet for new outdoor activities."[22] By the end of the nineteenth century the private lawn had taken on a parklike function.

The High Line's care of its Lawn uses no herbicides, pesticides or fungicides. Site-produced compost and compost teas are used to augment macro and micronutrients only as necessary. The Lawn is trimmed with a petroleum-fuel-free battery-powered mower. Despite this, the Lawn is unable to sustain the concentrated use it gets. In recent years it has been closed more than it's been open, allowing staff the work windows required for healing and regeneration.

The Lawn is another of the High Line's experiments. As intended, it inspires myriad unscripted responses to choreographed opportunity. Though formal in style it is one of the wildest places. The earthy appeal of its moist, living surface is undeniably sensual. Unlike artificial turf, real grass lawns—even the best of them—are imperfect.

Contradictory yet undeniably earthy, the Lawn is one of the High Line's wildest and most sensual places.

Day and night, the Seating Steps welcome all sorts of individual and community activity. In this October scene, the Lawn regenerates following another punishing season of *too much* love.

The Lawn is one of the High Line's delightful contradictions. Appearing incongruous in this early November aerial, it (*far right*) has nevertheless earned a place in the life of the High Line.

The sinuous curve of the Meadow Walk just north (*to the left*) of the Lawn is a designed departure from the straight path of the historic railroad tracks.

MEADOW WALK

West 23rd Street to West 25th Street

The twists and turns of the pathways are designed to put visitors in relationship to views.[23]

— JAMES CORNER

Those inclined to take the long way home know the most direct route between two points in the landscape isn't always the most illuminating. The Meadow Walk occupies a straight section of the former trackway and might have been a dull journey without the artful intervention of landscape architecture. As James Corner has observed: "The High Line was originally designed by engineers with a linear mindset—they wanted maximum efficiency, wanted the trains to run from A to B on a straight line."[24] Given the absence of varied topography—the Meadow Walk is entirely level—the most efficient way of directing visitors toward elements in the broader urban sphere is to keep the path at grade and vary the horizontal line. When such diversionary design elements are successfully implemented, their authorship is invisible and they seem like they were always there.

When the Meadow Walk opened in 2011 it was planted with mixed grasses including purple moor grass (*Molinia caerulea*) and Korean feather-reed grass (*Calamagrostis brachytricha*) and mixed broad-leaved perennial flowers including bright yellow fernleaf yarrow (*Achillea filipendulina* 'Parker's Variety'), Walker's Low catmint (*Nepeta racemosa* 'Walker's Low'), lesser calamint (*Calamintha nepeta*) and Full Moon tickseed (*Coreopsis* 'Full Moon'). In the ensuing years the feather-reed grass proved too well adapted to site conditions, self-seeding to the point of nearly overwhelming all companions. The yarrow persisted; however, most of the broad-leaved plants became dependent on the gardening staff's efforts to selectively remove excessive feather-reed grass seedlings. The relative vigor of the plant palette was out of balance.

Since adhering strictly to the initial design meant committing to unjustifiably high management cost, Piet Oudolf and the staff collaborated on artful yet practical updates, accepting the strength of the feather-reed grass as an asset and adding plants well matched to it. The introduction of blackberry-lily (*Belamcanda chinensis*) is a successful example. This sturdy perennial is widely recognized for its multiseason beauty but is often avoided due to its tendency to self-seed and overrun less energetic neighbors. It's well balanced with the feather-reed grass, and like it, is likely to persist even if construction along the High Line makes conditions on the Meadow Walk increasingly shady.

Though it's taken years to get from the point of initial planting to the present point in the Meadow Walk's evolution, the journey has been informed and enriched by its diversions. Sustainable design depends on identifying and nurturing functional relationships, and this often requires an enthusiasm for taking the long way home.

In late September, persistently beautiful seedheads of fernleaf yarrow (*Achillea filipendulina* 'Parker's Variety') and blackberry-lily (*Belamcanda chinensis*) add contrast to the dominant matrix of Korean feather-reed grass (*Calamagrostis brachytricha*).

Fernleaf yarrow blooms in June along with Walker's Low catmint (*Nepeta racemosa* 'Walker's Low') and blackberry-lily. The creatively curved pathway defines a deep planting space on the east side that has proved an ideal location for changing artwork.

Visitors unfamiliar with blackberry-lily might not associate the plant's bright orange summer flowers with the glossy black seed clusters they produce by early autumn (*opposite*).

Repurposed steel castings of
Marianne Vitale's *Common Crossings*
emerge strikingly from self-sustaining
sweeps of Korean feather-reed grass
in early November. Known as "frogs"
in the railroad industry, these single-cast
junctions allowed trains to cross tracks
without derailing. The begining of
the Flyover's elevated walkway is visible
in the distance.

FLYOVER

West 25th Street to West 27th Street

The Flyover was inspired by a memory. When the design team first explored the High Line in 2004, they discovered a tree-filled section closedly flanked by two tall buildings. Shade and protection from crosswinds had increased available moisture and created conditions capable of sustaining a virtual forest of ailanthus and mulberry trees. A raised loading platform along one of the buildings offered mid-canopy views. Despite the weedy nature of the two tree species, the experience made a lasting impression that would later be translated as the Flyover.

The Flyover's elevated walkway is a deliberate, radical departure from the High Line's level grade, and it serves multiple design purposes. It first becomes evident when strolling north through the Meadow Walk, adding intrigue to what could have been an over-long straight view and directing eyes upward to the towering architecture of the Hudson Yards project. Elevating the walk made it possible to create a varied topography below, with soil mounded deeply enough to support a virtual forest and an intricate mosaic of shrub and ground layer plantings. Short spurs along the walk seductively sideline visitors by offering seating in intimate rooms surrounded by the forest's organic architecture. Each of these spaces provides unique perspectives on the canopy and lower layers.

Though the Flyover forest includes redbuds, shadbush, sassafras and sumac, the great drama of its canopy is due to the dominant use of bigleaf magnolias, a suggestion by Patrick Cullina that the design team unanimously embraced. All native to eastern North America, the trees include the iconic bigleaf magnolia (*Magnolia macrophylla*), Ashe's magnolia (*M. macrophylla* var. *ashei*) and umbrella magnolia (*Magnolia tripetala*). The mix also includes the evergreen variety of sweetbay magnolia (*Magnolia virginiana* var. *australis* 'Green Shadow') which is smaller leaved but still bold-textured.

Diversity in the shrub and herbaceous layers is very high, yet the species composition is quite distinct from that of Chelsea Thicket and Gansevoort Woodland. The pageant of emerging growth in April and May is mesmerizing, as great drifts of ferns intermingle with sedges and broad-leaved flowering plants. Colors and textures morph through the growing season, then finish with a tapestry of harvest hues augmented by the fallen leaves of canopy trees.

When exiting the Flyover, visitors are first awed by the view north to 30th Street. Here, the walkway puts shadbush berries and magnolia flowers and seedpods within arm's reach before beginning its gentle descent to the sunny openness of the Wildflower Field.

Most of the High Line's special design moments were a response to the context. It's no coincidence that the Flyover happens between two buildings where trees were growing up to catch the light.[25] —LISA SWITKIN

The Flyover's elevated walkway immerses visitors in the canopy layer and provides top-down views to the rich mosaic of the shrub and ground layers.

The experience of a forest is on the one hand immense—you're lost, it's massive
—and on the other hand it's intimate because everything is so close and so tactile.[26]
—JAMES CORNER

Eastern North American bigleaf magnolias are the signature of the Flyover forest's canopy layer. Attaining full size by early June, the leaves' exceedingly bold texture conjures the prehistoric landscapes that gave birth to modern-day magnolias. Bigleaf magnolia (*Magnolia macrophylla*) flowers open in May, morph into sculptural pink pods by late summer, then display seeds for dispersal in autumn.

The Flyover includes a special viewing spur as the High Line crosses 26th Street. The spur's lighted frame invites visitors to relax on a reclined wood bench, day or night, contemplating skyline and the view east through the varied architecture of West Chelsea.

Berries of red baneberry (*Actaea pachypoda*) stand out among the mature midsummer green hues of ferns and mixed broad-leaved herbaceous companions carpeting the ground layer.

Maidenhair fern (*Adiantum pedatum*) retains some of its springtime brightness, complementing the berries' saturated color.

Opposite: Often within arm's reach along the Flyover walkway, the edible berries of shadbush rival blueberries in their sweetness.

Delicate sky-blue flowers and boldly variegated leaves of Jack Frost Siberian bugloss (*Brunnera macrophylla* 'Jack Frost') enrich the Flyover's ground layer in April and May.

Silver-haired new fronds of Christmas fern (*Polystichum acrostichoides*) and delicate orange-red stalks of maidenhair fern are illuminated by April sunlight streaming across the mounded ground-scape below the Flyover's elevated walkway.

Native azaleas including coastal azalea (*Rhododendron atlanticum*) and swamp azalea (*Rhododendron viscosum*) and fallen leaves of canopy trees contribute harvest colors to the autumn ground layer. Dark green foliage of dwarf mondo grass (*Ophiopogon japonicus* 'Nana') and Allegheny pachysandra (*Pachysandra procumbens*) stands out from the lighter green of sedges, Hakone grass and maidenhair ferns.

Mitten-shaped sassafras leaves take on apricot and burnt umber tones as winged sumac (*Rhus copallinum*) (*opposite*) turns crimson in autumn, flanking the Flyover's descent toward the Wildflower Field.

WILDFLOWER FIELD & RADIAL PLANTINGS

West 27th Street to West 30th Street

The Wildflower Field is the final stretch in a revelatory journey north through alternating woodlands and grasslands, intimacy and immensity. In a way it is one of the simplest garden spaces, consisting of a long, level run devoted to multiseason displays of colorful perennial flowers. Its extended straightaway is reminiscent of the uninterrupted vistas of the unreconstructed High Line and is most powerful when viewed from the Flyover's elevation. In a different way it is a space of great complexity and tension. The Wildflower Field's transition to the dramatic curve of the Radial Plantings is visible from great distance and is inseparable from the terminal view of disorientingly tall new buildings. Though near-constant construction has become the norm along much of the High Line, the nexus of activity just beyond the Radial Plantings is the most spectacular evidence of a city in flux. In mind and mood, the serenity and human scale of the plantings and the monumental scale of things to come are powerful juxtapositions.

Grasses mostly play supporting roles in these gardens—broad-leaved flowering plants are the stars here. A few of them, including North American natives prairie sage (*Salvia azurea*), tall tickseed (*Coreopsis tripteris*) and willowleaf sunflower (*Helianthus salicifolius*), are unusually tall, attaining heights of six to eight feet by midsummer. They tower above grasses including prairie dropseed and sideoats grama (*Bouteloua curtipendula*), contributing strong vertical presence that is more typically achieved with shrubs or small trees. The rich mix of flowering species, both native and exotic, makes this one of the best places to observe birds, bees and butterflies. They begin visiting in April as crocuses bloom and continue in May as ornamental onions (*Allium nigrum* and *Allium christophii*) native to sunny Middle Eastern regions bloom with foxtail lilies (*Eremurus himalaicus*) from the western Himalayas. In June and July they visit North American coneflowers (*Echinacea purpurea* and *Echinacea pallida*), then continue into autumn, attracted by late-blooming asters, blazing stars and showy goldenrod (*Solidago speciosa*), and by the seeds of many different species.

The Radial Plantings follow the original route of the railway: a long gentle curve to the left that ends with the High Line facing west to the Hudson River. A radial bench borders the plantings on the west side, offering generous room for relaxing individually or in groups. Karl Foerster's feather-reed grass (*Calamagrostis ×acutiflora* 'Karl Foerster') mixes with big sweeps of coneflowers here, moving with every summer breeze and autumn wind, adding to the dynamics and anticipating the head-turning spectacle of the Rail Yards.

Azure-blue-flowered prairie sage (*Salvia azurea*) and tall tickseed (*Coreopsis tripteris*) tower over prairie dropseed, reaching heights of six to eight feet by midsummer.

Opposite: Flower spikes of foxtail lilies (*Eremurus himalaicus*) from the western Himalayas rise above low grasses in May, blooming along with white-flowered ornamental onion (*Allium nigrum*) and star of Persia (*Allium christophii*), a lavender-flowered onion that is also native to sunny Middle Eastern regions.

A red admiral butterfly takes nectar from *Allium nigrum*, a Middle Eastern native known variously as ornamental onion, black garlic, or broad-leaved garlic.

A century ago wildflowers were commonly refered to as wild flowers. The two-word form put the emphasis on wild, and the definition included shrubs and trees that were wild and flowered. With this in mind, lead plant (*Amorpha canescens*) is a fitting inclusion in the Wildflower Field. Native to open woodlands, glades and prairies in central North America, it is uncommon in cultivation but has thrived on the High Line.

Below, in foreground, flowering stalks of foxtail lily become seed stalks as lead plant blooms in late June.

Prairie smoke (*Geum triflorum*) flowers mature to plumy seedheads in late May.

Pale coneflower (*Echinacea pallida*) attracts bees and other pollinators in June.

Karl Foerster's feather-reed grass
(*Calamagrostis* ×*acutiflora* 'Karl Foerster')
emerges from purple coneflowers
(*Echinacea purpurea*) in mid-July.

NICKEL

Karl Foerster's feather-reed grass and Korean feather-reed grass dance around seedheads of purple coneflower in late September as showy goldenrod (*Solidago speciosa*) blooms.

Opposite: Showy goldenrod seedheads stand upright in November.

RAIL YARDS

West 30th Street to West 34th Street

In America, the last frontier has always been to the west, so it's fitting that the High Line's last frontier is at the Rail Yards, extending west toward the Hudson River. A mighty imagination is required to envision conditions on the High Line as it runs the perimeter of the rail yard site a decade from now, which is why Friends of the High Line opted to build the Interim Walkway: a brilliant yet practical journey into the unknown. It's a temporary solution, "long-term temporary"[27] as Lisa Switkin has mused, since it could be fifteen years or more before the yards are completely transformed into Hudson Yards, the largest private real estate development in U.S. history.

The High Line at the Rail Yards is a multifaceted affair. The curve north through the Radial Plantings joins the 'Line at an extra-wide landing point designed to accommodate thousands of Hudson Yards residents and visitors streaming in daily. Just east of this, gardens on the spur over 10th Avenue have been designed to offer wooded enclosure as well as breathtaking views in all directions. Plantings adjacent to the landing point and continuing west over 11th Avenue include a diversity of low grasses and flowering perennials and an open canopy of Kentucky coffee trees (*Gymnocladus dioicus*). This is one of the High Line's most playful places, where the young at heart can teach the young in years how to walk the top of a steel track.

The redesigned portion of the High Line at the Rail Yards ends beyond 11th Avenue at the beginning of the Interim Walkway. Though distinctly different than the original railroad landscape, both sections preserve the historic materials, aesthetics and human scale that characterize the sections south of the yards. After careful consideration, Friends of the High Line and the design team decided this approach would provide the one thread that's consistent through the journey running south to north, from brick and iron to steel and glass. In terms of design drama, they decided keeping it constant would be the most surreal thing they could do.

The Interim Walkway is another great ecological experiment. The self-seeded wild plants and associated faunal communities that ring the Rail Yards are being left to their own devices. Descendants of wildlings that claimed the landscape after the trains quit the tracks, they continue in vigorous response to changing conditions. For the next many years, human visitors will be able to observe the various habitats on display, contemplating subtle changes in pattern and composition. This is the beauty of wildness. Wildness is regenerative. Wildness is a renewable resource.

The Rail Yards is the High Line's final frontier in geography only, since conceptually there is no end to the High Line. The spontaneity built into its design ethos ensures it will constantly reinvent itself in a never-ending celebration of living process.

The Interim Walkway heads west to the Hudson, then skirts the periphery of the historic West Side Rail Yards before descending to grade at 34th Street.

The Rail Yards' redesign continues the High Line's celebration of its rail origins, its naturalism and human scale.

Top: The chance to practice one's balance is open to anyone still young at heart.

Bottom: Spinners geranium (*Geranium* 'Spinners') provides nectar for visiting bees from late spring into early summer.

Opposite: Foxglove beardtongue (*Penstemon digitalis*) softens edges along a section of track.

Top: Observers enjoy elevated views of the Hudson as Queen Anne's lace (*Daucus carota*), a newly native New Yorker, thrives in the wildscape ringing the Rail Yards.

Bottom: Sweetly fragrant common milkweed (*Asclepias syriaca*) is an essential stopover for migrating monarch butterflies.

Top: Siberian crabapple (*Malus baccata*) has been living its life on the 'Line for decades, unwatered but not unwanted by pollinating insects and nesting birds.

Bottom: Among eastern North American native trees, black cherry (*Prunus serotina*) is near the top of the list for sustaining wildlife. Doug Tallamy's research documents its role as host plant for over 400 butterfly and moth species.

All tracks paralleling the Interim Walkway are undisturbed, resting on the same wooden "sleepers" (ties) that have held them in place since the time the trains were running. The foundry origins of many are cast in steel.

Seed stalks of common evening primrose (*Oenothera biennis*) and flannel plant (*Verbascum thapsus*) rise above drifts of tall thoroughwort (*Eupatorium altissimum*) in October.

Opposite: The Rail Yards' unreconstructed wildscape can't match the seasonal dynamics of the planted sections, but it does have its moments. In November, black cherry, Siberian crabapple and oriental bittersweet (*Celastrus orbiculatus*) add color to cloudlike masses of prairie threeawn (*Aristida oligantha*).

Common milkweed throws caution to the wind, dispersing seeds that hold the promise of future generations.

A helicopter view of the Rail Yards in late October, showing the High Line's last half mile running from 30th Street (*left*) to 34th Street. Though the tracks will all be covered by development, the Walkway's views to the river will be preserved.

Gardening

Owned by the City of New York, the High Line is a public park maintained, operated and programmed by Friends of the High Line in partnership with the New York City Department of Parks and Recreation. Each year Friends of the High Line raises all of the funds and provides all of the personnel required to care for its gardens.

The High Line's gardens break from tradition in countless ways, and as a result their care requires a different type of gardening performed by a different breed of gardeners. Traditional gardens are designed primarily to be decorative, relying on fixed planting patterns that are, by nature, static. Their care is devoted to preserving the existing state of affairs—the status quo—and such care is properly called maintenance. Though the High Line's gardens are beautiful, their design is based upon dynamic rather than fixed patterns. Their existing state of affairs is a moving target. Caring for these ever-changing gardens involves artful stewardship, not maintenance. There is no status quo on the High Line.

One of the greatest challenges has been gardeners' limited access to plantings and equipment. In traditional gardens, planted areas are typically bordered by broad paved surfaces or surrounded by turf, making it easy to pull carts or motorized vehicles close to work areas. Within planted areas, extensive use of mulch often makes it easy to walk in-between plants without trampling them. In contrast, the High Line's narrow pathways make powered vehicles largely impractical and the density of plant cover makes balancing on tiptoes through beds more of a dance than a walk. Combine this with a near-continual public presence, remote access to support facilities, and the need to carry virtually all tools and materials to and from the gardens' elevation and it becomes clear how unique conditions are.

The initial planting of the gardens was completed before they were opened to the public. Following remediation of the High Line's historic structure, planting areas were filled with new soil and drip irrigation was installed. In areas with mixed tree, shrub and herbaceous layers, the larger woody plants were placed first, followed by smaller shrubs, grasses and perennials. All plants selected were judged likely to thrive in their new site conditions, though since the exact nature of those conditions would be revealed over time, plant selection necessarily involved significant experimentation. The High Line is in many ways like a continuous green roof. Shallow soil depth, extreme summer heat and winter cold, and repeated freezing and thawing create conditions that test the resilience of even the hardiest plants.

All along the 'Line, the herbaceous layer was planted with a mix of clump-forming and running species. Many of the clump-formers were known not to be self-seeders. These would increase in size but not in number. Other clump-formers such as prairie dropseed (*Sporobolus heterolepis*) were expected to self-seed, filling interstices and eventually creating continuous

Gardener Kevin Williams observes and edits the herbaceous layer of the Wildflower Field. Such work requires an experienced eye and an understanding of plant community dynamics. Photo by Amelia Holowaty Krales.

cover. Running species such as mountain mint (*Pycnanthemum muticum*) were expected to increase their spread by means of underground stems, eventually touching neighboring plants but, ideally, not overpowering them.

Spaces in-between plants were initially mulched with gray gravel. Intended to evoke the ballast stone that once held railroad ties in place, the gravel succeeded visually but has complicated the tasks of weeding, dividing and transplanting, increasing the time required for these activities. In response, gardeners are increasingly focused on using plants as living mulch in place of the gravel.

The High Line's soils were initially formulated to provide the structure, drainage, acidity, organic matter and nutrients required to support a broad array of woody and herbaceous plants. Since that time, compost produced on site from material harvested during the cutback has been regularly applied to replenish soil organic matter and fertility. Beginning more recently, site-produced compost teas are applied to enrich the soil population of beneficial organisms. The gardening staff is increasingly dedicated to preserving the roles soil organisms play in sustaining plant health. As gardener Erin Eck explains: "Many people think of soil as being inert, rather than as a living system. When we add compost, we provide food for soil organisms. When we apply compost tea, we increase the population of beneficial organisms. Since they're involved in everything from defense against pathogens to making nutrients available to plants, they need our support."

Gardening on the High Line is based on an ethic of observation, and staff, interns and volunteers are continually alert for subtle cues to changes that may require further attention or intervention. Because the plants are not arranged in fixed patterns, replacement in kind may not be the best response when a plant fails. Gardeners observe and analyze circumstances that are likely to have caused plants to weaken or die, looking closely for changing dynamics in the relationships between plants and their neighbors.

A failing plant may indicate the species or cultivated variety isn't adapted to specific site conditions, and in this case a more suitable replacement is sought. The substitution of little bluestem cultivar 'Standing Ovation' for 'The Blues' is an example. In other cases the problem may be due to a mismatch in the vigor of neighboring plant communities, and the most resource-conserving fix may require revising the design.

Melissa Fisher, then Deputy Director of Horticulture for Friends of the High Line, inspects new initial plantings in September 2008.

The nuanced nature of Piet Oudolf's approach anticipates rearrangements of patterns in response to changing biological dynamics, so when such situations are revealed the staff and Oudolf collaborate on effective design solutions. As gardener Erin Eck describes the process: "Piet designs for change over both the short term and long term. Some changes he has planned for and some he hasn't. As a gardener you have to be able to anticipate the form a planting will take over the course of years. When he visits, Piet often reminds us to resist the desire for total control. It's very important that a sense of wildness comes through."

Becoming comfortable with the flux and developing the confidence to embrace change are skills Friends of the High Line gardeners learn from their work. Eck remembers how her initial frustration with self-seeding Korean feather-reed grass gave way to admiration, saying "I was spending so much time weeding its seedlings out of neighboring plants that Piet teased me about it, asking if I'd made my peace with that grass. Now I sort of admire its vigor. I can count on it to grow happily in places where other plants struggle."

From the point of view of resource conservation, it is less consuming and more sustainable to selectively remove excessive vigor than to continually replace plants that are poorly adapted to conditions. In keeping with this, much of what the gardeners do is best described as editing or as addition by reduction. Additional functionality results from the reductive process of selective removal. As Friends of the High Line Director of Horticulture Andi Pettis summarizes, "Plantings on the High Line mimic the dynamics of wild landscapes and are

Tracks and ties have been re-laid, the bed has been filled with new soil, and planting of the Wildflower Field is underway in October 2010, prior to this section's opening to the public.

meant to change. Plants outcompete one another, spread, or diminish. They drift in the environment to where they can best fill niches. Our work is to facilitate and enhance processes of growth, change and movement while maintaining the integrity of the design."

The practice of editing also applies to trees and shrubs. Though they are less likely to self-sow as prolifically as herbaceous plants, woody plants frequently outgrow their allotted niches or increase so much in size that they threaten the balance of the design. Outsized trees and shrubs can also negatively impact the growth of understory plants by shading them or creating excessive competition for moisture in rooting zones.

Managing the High Line's woody plants requires artful pruning. In many cases pruning is an incremental, ongoing process. In others, an effective technique is to cut the plant to the ground periodically in the knowledge that healthy new stems will sprout from the base. Grace smokebush (*Cotinus* 'Grace') is an example of a shrub that may be managed in this way. Many trees that are inclined to multistemmed growth, such as gray birch (*Betula populifolia*), will respond to the selective removal of older growth by producing new stems from the base.

Andi Pettis (current Director of Horticulture for Friends of the High Line) and Johnny Linville make subtle adjustments to the Northern Spur plant community. Photo by Patrick Cullina.

Editing may prove equally applicable to the still-wild plant communities of the Rail Yards' Interim Walkway. Ostensibly this area is not gardened: it isn't planted, weeded or watered but is instead left to evolve without deliberate intervention. The problem with this perspective is that it doesn't take unintended intervention into account. Rain falling on the Interim Walkway drains into the vegetation, and fencing erected for safety reasons slows windspeed and reduces evapotranspiration rates. The combined result is that available moisture has been greatly increased, and this is having a significant effect on the spontaneous plant community that originally developed in response to extremely dry conditions.

Plants with the capacity to endure drought are losing the competitive advantage they once enjoyed, and new species adapted to higher moisture levels are beginning to dominate. Callery pears (*Pyrus calleryana*), recorded as rare in Richard Stalter's 2004 Torrey Botanical Society article "The Flora on the High Line, New York City, New York"[28] are now self-seeding with abandon, and some are already over head height. Introduced to the United States from China in the 1950s for decorative purposes, this tree has naturalized in more than half the states, including New York. It's both a pernicious weed that threatens regional ecosystems and a multiseason ornamental tree perfectly adapted to modern urban conditions. Unless action is taken, Walkway vegetation could be dominated by pears and oriental bittersweet within a decade. Intervention will be needed to affect a different outcome, and if it is undertaken, it will then make sense to recognize the formerly wild community as a managed garden.

Intern Ayinde Listhrop and gardener Yuki Kaneko gently exit the Northern Spur on tiptoe after making a few select edits to the plantings.

Top: Senior gardener John Gunderson makes countless decisions while pruning to ensure the health and artful form of gray birches in Gansevoort Woodland.

Lower left: Senior gardener Kasper Wittlinger makes subtle edits around the Sundeck.

Lower right: Gardener Erin Eck readies plants that will become part of the living ground cover below sumacs in the Hudson River Overlook.

The concept of ecological succession has relevance for the High Line's gardens. Succession was once envisioned as a sequence of stages on the way to an eventual climax—an ultimate equilibrium. In the classic model, lichens break down rock, soil develops, pioneering grasses pave the way for woody plants and eventually a climax forest lives happily ever after. It's now understood that ecological processes are continually re-set in small and large increments, and that stasis is a temporal illusion. Gardeners typically interrupt successional process to allow the landscape to remain in a desired stage. Gardeners in northeastern North America who choose not to intervene generally wind up with a shade garden. On the High Line, increasing shade is due to increasing growth of tall buildings, not tall trees. Some of the gardens will always be sunny. Others will undergo incremental change, remaining beautiful and functional as their layers and composition evolve to make the most of new conditions.

Caring for the complexity and diversity of the High Line's landscape is an uncommon experience in the realm of modern parks and public gardens. Each working day, gardeners learn new ways to improve their powers of observation and analysis. The work requires a non-standard amalgam of horticulture, ecology, soil science, entomology, ornithology and artistry. Those who spend time at it are attending a virtual school of urban landscape stewardship. Providing such experience is one of the many ways the High Line's gardens elevate the nature of modern landscapes and the community of people entrusted with their care.

Gardener Nathan Bartholomew contemplates a ten-foot tall callery pear (*Pyrus calleryana*) seedling thriving in the wild community bordered by the Rail Yard's Interim Walkway.

Life Line

The New York Central Railroad began construction of the elevated West Side Line in 1931, predicting it "will have lasting beneficial and fundamental effects on the life and well-being of the city and its people."[29] When completed in 1934 it was Manhattan Island's only all-rail freight line, built to transport milk, butter, eggs, meat and cheese from upstate farms into the city, and it soon became known as the Life Line of New York. In ways unimaginable to engineers and architects of the 1930s, that same vital corridor is now a life line of a different sort, enriching the lives of the city's human and non-human residents and visitors.

When the tracks went quiet in the 1980s and '90s, avian urban explorers scoured the regenerating railscape for seeds and berries, for materials to make nests and protected niches in which to build them. Bumblebees burrowed below the ballast, emerging to gather pollen. Caterpillars munched on leaves, morphed into moths and butterflies, and sought nectar from wild flowers. Vegetation was sparse and life was hard, but even so it was much easier for wildlife to make a living here than from the streets below. When, after nearly three decades of dereliction, the trackway was transformed into a series of biologically diverse gardens, the abundance and diversity of life on the 'Line exploded in response.

Nearly 400 species of plants now grow on the High Line, supporting, in various ways, a multitude of resident and migratory birds—catbirds, mockingbirds, kinglets, tanagers, orioles, grosbeaks, woodpeckers, flickers, hawks, doves, sparrows, robins, ravens, cardinals, finches and warblers—and bees, bugs, moths, flies, butterflies, dragonflies, crickets and spiders. Thanks to enlightened stewardship, floral-faunal relationships are recognized and supported, and all denizens enjoy an environment free from herbicides and insecticides. Beauty is regularly redefined to include all stages of the carbon cycle, knowing that life depends upon it.

The High Line is far from providing universal habitat. It includes no true wetlands, swamps or bogs. It has its dry moments but nothing equaling the searing drought of eastern barrens. Its mostly level terrain includes no cliff faces or rocky crags. The narrowness of its corridor is an inherent limiter for species that require wide expanses of forested canopy. What it does provide is a model of beautiful, meaningful, purposeful habitat worthy of emulation in other parks, greenways and residential landscapes. Its story is one of resilience and resourcefulness and of individual dreams leading to vibrant civic accomplishment.

Blazing star (*Liatris scariosa*) provides nectar to a painted lady butterfly in mid-July.

Top left: A honeybee collects pollen and nectar from purple prairie clover (*Dalea pupurea*) in June.

Top center: Aromatic aster is visited by a bumblebee in October.

Top right: Purple coneflower provides pollen to a megachile leafcutter bee in June.

Bottom right and left: In June, close observation is required to spot a cabbage looper on the colorful flowers of

Rubinzwerg sneezeweed (*Helenium* 'Rubinzwerg').

Within ten minutes of a June visit to the High Line, I witnessed three monarchs and three species of bees all taking nectar and pollen from a single butterfly milkweed. This hopeful sight provided living

Top left and right: Claire Grace bergamot (*Monarda fistulosa* 'Claire Grace') attracts painted lady butterflies in May.

Bottom right: A bumblebee approaches a yellow hybrid coneflower in June.

Bottom center: A monarch takes nectar from butterfly milkweed (*Asclepias tuberosa*) in June. Photo by Doug Tallamy.

Bottom left: Aromatic aster is visited by a monarch in October.

Left center: Milkweed bugs congregate on top of a light fixture in November.

proof that the High Line's plantings play a genuine role in sustaining essential ecological relationships.

— DOUG TALLAMY

Top left: Sparrows balance on flower stalks of prairie dock (*Silphium terebinthinaceum*) in October.

Top right: A mockingbird sings atop coral honeysuckle (*Lonicera sempervirens* 'Major Wheeler') and American bittersweet (*Celastrus scandens* 'Bailumn') in November.

Right center: A baby mockingbird peeks from its home at the Rail Yards. Photo by Steven Severinghaus.

Right bottom: A palm warbler forages at the Rail Yards. Photo by Steven Severinghaus.

Left bottom: A yellow-bellied sapsucker alights on a redbud in February. Photo by Erika Harvey, Friends of the High Line.

Top left: House finches share food with a kiss amid shadbush flower buds. Photo by Steven Severinghaus.

Top right: Dawn viburnum (*Viburnum xbodnantense* 'Dawn') provides a perch for a white-throated sparrow. Photo by Mike Tschappat.

Bottom right: A mockingbird feasts on winterberry holly (*Ilex verticillata*). Photo by Mike Tschappat.

Bottom left: Aster seeds sustain a ruby-crowned kinglet on the Northern Spur in late October.

Left center: A sparrow feeds on juicy berries of black choke-berry (*Aronia melanocarpa* 'Viking'). Photo by Steven Severinghaus.

Seasons

Children growing up in temperate northeastern North America are taught to count only four seasons, and this is simply wrong. Anyone of any age who rejects this convention knows there are as many seasons as the mind's eye can discern. Is it sensible to recognize a season of icy seedheads or a season of long shadows, a season of new greens or a season of unfurling fronds? Celebration of fleeting, barely perceptible events in the landscape's living cycle is absolutely sensible and profoundly sensual. With each recognition comes the ability to see more deeply, and with this a world of beautiful, meaningful detail is continually revealed. These revelations are incidental keys to universal processes.

The passings of seasons large and small, long and short, account for the greatest dramas of the High Line's gardens, and a sensitivity to ephemera is elemental to the ethos of their design. Japanese culture recognizes this as *mono no aware*, which may be translated as the awareness of impermanence or the inevitable transience of all things. The concept accommodates a gentle lament for passings but is primarily focused on the notion that awareness of the transitory nature of existence is all the more reason to celebrate each present moment as a gift.

The gardens' free access invites frequent and spontaneous visits, and the complexity of their layering ensures there'll always be worlds of detail awaiting discovery. Contrary to the increasing *push* of digital technology, the gardens remain a decidedly *pull* medium. No visitor is pushed to record the number of days redbud blossoms require to open, or how long they remain colorful after falling to the ground, but all visitors are free to pull such insights from experience. Fall in love with last year's coneflower, ice-capped in February, and the bud-to-bloom details of its floral morphology will be on full display beginning in May. The emerging stems of maidenhair fern are so coiled, so slight and so strongly red-brown in color it's hard to imagine they can transform themselves into bright green fluttering fronds held aloft on ebony black stalks—unless you take time to bear witness.

Despite, or perhaps because of the fixity of its peripheral architecture, the High Line is an intensely seasonal landscape. Changing sky colors and moods reflect off glass and steel, off woods and grass, inviting capture with a sharp lens or sharp eyes. Contemplative visitors know to watch the layers—vertical, temporal and cultural—entwining to endless effect as moments pass in the seasons of the gardens' living characters.

It's not what you see, but what you see in it. It's not a flower arrangement. It's something original and organic. It plays on the senses, and that is its strength. When choosing the living "characters" in my designs, the structure and sculptural quality of each plant are more important than flowers or color. — PIET OUDOLF

After a February snowstorm, ice-capped seedheads of purple coneflower stand tall enough to cast long shadows.

In April, new fronds of maidenhair fern (*Adiantum pedatum*) begin as fragile coils, their red-brown color bearing no resemblance to the bright green hue they'll attain by May.

The flowers and foliage in the background belong to Eurasian fumewort (*Corydalis solida*), a true spring ephemeral that goes completely dormant by late spring. In contrast, the maidenhair fern remains green and persists until late autumn.

Sunset and silhouettes of a July evening are a reminder that understanding the mood of many moments warrants a skyward glance.

Opposite: The resting beauty of bigleaf magnolia leaves constitutes a season worthy of recognition.

For me, garden design
is not just about plants,
it is about emotion,
atmosphere, a sense of
contemplation.
You try to move people
with what you do.
That is the big part.
A garden isn't a landscape
painting that you
look at, but a dynamic
process that's always
changing. You must keep
in touch with it all
of the time.

—PIET OUDOLF

The sculptural qualities of Marianne
Vitale's *Common Crossings* are
enhanced by a heavy snowstorm
in early March.

ENDNOTES

1. From September 4, 2013, discussion with Isabel Castilla, James Corner, Rick Darke, Annik La Farge, and Lisa Switkin; transcribed by Annik La Farge.

2. Adam Gopnick, "A Walk on the High Line," *The New Yorker* (May 21, 2001).

3. Gaston Bachelard, *The Poetics of Space* (Boston: Beacon Press, 1969), 61.

4. Gaston Bachelard, *The Poetics of Space* (Boston: Beacon Press, 1969), 183.

5. James Corner Field Operations and Diller Scofidio + Renfro. *The High Line* (New York: Phaidon Press, 2015).

6. William Robinson, *The Wild Garden* (London: John Murray, 1870).

7. William Robinson, *The Wild Garden* (London: John Murray, 1870), 16:2.

8. Karl Foerster, *Einzug der Gräser und Farne in die Gärten* (Radebeul, Germany: Neumann Verlag, 1957).

9. Richard Stalter, "The Flora on the High Line, New York City, New York," *Journal of the Torrey Botanical Society* 131, no. 4 (October–December 2004).

10. James Corner Field Operations and Diller Scofidio + Renfro. *The High Line* (New York: Phaidon Press, 2015).

11. James Corner Field Operations and Diller Scofidio + Renfro. *The High Line* (New York: Phaidon Press, 2015).

12. Ingo Kowarik and Stefan Körner, *Wild Urban Woodlands* (Belin: Springer, 2005), 290.

13. Piet Oudolf and Henk Gerritsen, *Droomplanten: de Nieuwe Generatie Tuinplaten* (Houten, Netherlands: Terra, 1990).

14. Paula Scher, "Great Design Is Serious, Not Solemn" (TED talk for the Art Center Design Conference, May 2008).

15. James Corner Field Operations and Diller Scofidio + Renfro. *The High Line* (New York: Phaidon Press, 2015).

16. James Corner Field Operations and Diller Scofidio + Renfro. "The High Line Phase 1 Report" (unpublished, 2005).

17. James Corner Field Operations and Diller Scofidio + Renfro. *The High Line* (New York: Phaidon Press, 2015).

18. James Corner Field Operations and Diller Scofidio + Renfro. *The High Line* (New York: Phaidon Press, 2015).

19. James Corner Field Operations and Diller Scofidio + Renfro. *The High Line* (New York: Phaidon Press, 2015).

20. New York Central Lines, *West Side Improvement: Initial Stage Dedicated June 28, 1934,* pamphlet.

21. James Corner Field Operations and Diller Scofidio + Renfro. *The High Line* (New York: Phaidon Press, 2015).

22. Kenneth Jackson, *Crabgrass Frontier: The Suburbanization of the United States* (New York: Oxford University Press, 1985).

23. From September 4, 2013, discussion with Isabel Castilla, James Corner, Rick Darke, Annik La Farge, and Lisa Switkin; transcribed by Annik La Farge.

24. From September 4, 2013, discussion with Isabel Castilla, James Corner, Rick Darke, Annik La Farge, and Lisa Switkin; transcribed by Annik La Farge.

25. From September 4, 2013, discussion with Isabel Castilla, James Corner, Rick Darke, Annik La Farge, and Lisa Switkin; transcribed by Annik La Farge.

26. From September 4, 2013, discussion with Isabel Castilla, James Corner, Rick Darke, Annik La Farge, and Lisa Switkin; transcribed by Annik La Farge.

27. From September 4, 2013, discussion with Isabel Castilla, James Corner, Rick Darke, Annik La Farge, and Lisa Switkin; transcribed by Annik La Farge.

28. Richard Stalter, "The Flora on the High Line, New York City, New York," *Journal of the Torrey Botanical Society* 131, no. 4 (October–December 2004) 392.

29. New York Central Lines, *West Side Improvement: Initial Stage Dedicated June 28, 1934,* pamphlet.

SUGGESTED READING

Bachelard, Gaston. *The Poetics of Space*. Boston: Beacon Press, 1969.

Darke, Rick. *The American Woodland Garden: Capturing the Spirit of the Deciduous Forest*. Portland: Timber Press, 2002.

Darke, Rick. *The Encyclopedia of Grasses for Livable Landscapes*. Portland: Timber Press, 2007.

Darke, Rick, and Doug Tallamy. *The Living Landscape: Designing for Beauty and Biodiversity in the Home Garden*. Portland: Timber Press, 2014.

David, Joshua, and Robert Hammond. *High Line: The Inside Story of New York City's Park in the Sky*. New York: Farrar, Straus and Giroux, 2011.

Jackson, Kenneth. *Crabgrass Frontier: The Suburbanization of the United States*. New York: Oxford University Press, 1985.

James Corner Field Operations and Diller Scofidio + Renfro. *The High Line*. New York: Phaidon Press, 2015.

Kingsbury, Noel, and Piet Oudolf. *Planting: A New Perspective*. Portland: Timber Press, 2013.

Kowarik, Ingo, and Stefan Körner. *Wild Urban Woodlands*. Berlin: Springer, 2005.

La Farge, Annik. *On the High Line: Exploring America's Most Original Urban Park*. New York: Thames & Hudson, 2014.

Oudolf, Piet, and Henk Gerritsen. *Dream Plants for the Natural Garden*. Portland: Timber Press, 2000.

Oudolf, Piet, and Noel Kingsbury. *Oudolf Hummelo: A Journey Through a Plantsman's Life*. New York: The Monacelli Press, 2015.

Robinson, William, and Rick Darke. *The Wild Garden: Expanded Edition*. Portland: Timber Press, 2010.

Stalter, Richard. "The Flora on the High Line, New York City, New York." *Journal of the Torrey Botanical Society* 131, no. 4 (October–December 2004), 387–393.

Sternfeld, Joel. *Walking the High Line*. Göttingen: Steidl, 2001.

Stilgoe, John. *Borderland: Origins of the American Suburb, 1829–1939*. New Haven: Yale University Press, 1988.

Stilgoe, John. *Outside Lies Magic: Regaining History and Awareness in Everyday Places*. New York: Walker and Company, 1998.

ACKNOWLEDGMENTS

We wouldn't have had anything to write about if not for Friends of the High Line, the remarkable organization founded in 1999 by Robert Hammond and Joshua David that provided the vision, assembled the design team, developed support, implemented construction, and now manages and operates the park, and raises all of the funds and provides all of the personnel required to care for the High Line's gardens. We are grateful to so many Friends of the High Line staff, board members, patrons and volunteers who shared their knowledge, and give special thanks to staff members Andi Pettis, Erin Eck, Erika Harvey, John Gunderson, Kaspar Wittlinger, Nathan Bartholomew and Yuki Kaneko.

This book would not have been possible without the generous contributions of the following individuals, organizations and institutions: Joel Sternfeld and Luhring Augustine, New York; James Corner, Lisa Switkin and all at James Corner Field Operations; Matthew Johnson and all at Diller Scofidio + Renfro; Paula Scher; Phaidon Press; Whitney Museum of American Art; Gifford Miller; Elizabeth Gilmore; Patrick Cullina; Tom Smarr; Melissa Fisher; Annik La Farge; Steven Severinghaus; Barry Munger; Doug Tallamy; Mike Tschappat; Melinda Zoehrer; and Jeff Bennett.

INDEX

Published in 2017
by Timber Press, Inc.

The Haseltine Building
133 S.W. Second Avenue, Suite 450
Portland, Oregon 97204-3527
timberpress.com

Photography
Rick Darke and Piet Oudolf
unless otherwise noted

Design
Lorraine Ferguson

Cartography
Marty Schnure

Printed in China
Second printing 2019

ISBN 13: 978-1-60469-699-8

Catalog records for this
book are available from the
Library of Congress and
the British Library.